FOLKSONGS
FOR
UKULELE

ISBN 978-1-4234-6762-5

HAL•LEONARD®
CORPORATION

7777 W. BLUEMOUND RD. P.O. BOX 13819 MILWAUKEE, WI 53213

In Australia Contact:
Hal Leonard Australia Pty. Ltd
4 Lentara Court
Cheltenham, Victoria, 3192 Australia
Email: ausadmin@halleonard.com.au

Visit Hal Leonard Online at
www.halleonard.com

CONTENTS

All Through the Night

Welsh Folksong

First note

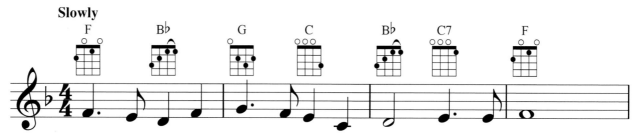

1. Sleep,   my child, and   peace   at-tend Thee,   all   through   the   night;
2. While   the moon her   watch   is keep-ing,   all   through   the   night;
3. You,   my God,   a   Babe   of won - der,   all   through   the   night;

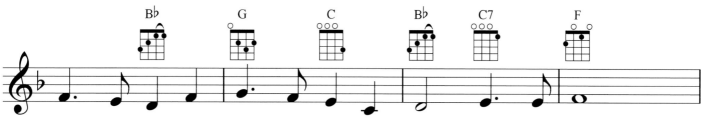

guard - ian   an - gels   God   will   send Thee,   all   through   the   night.
while   the   wea - ry   world   is   sleep - ing,   all   through   the   night.
dreams   You dream can't   break   from   thun - der,   all   through   the   night.

Soft   the   drows - y   hours are   creep - ing,   hill   and   vale   in   slum - ber   sleep - ing.
Through your   dreams you're   swift - ly   steal - ing,   vi - sions   of   de - light   re - veal - ing,
Chil - dren's dreams   can - not   be   bro - ken;   life   is   but   a   love - ly   to - ken.

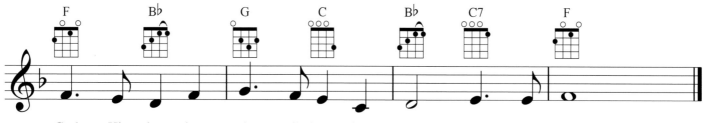

God   His   lov - ing   vig - il keep - ing,   all   through   the   night.
Christ - mas - time   is   so   ap - peal - ing,   all   through   the   night.
Christ - mas   should   be   soft - ly   spo - ken,   all   through   the   night.

Amazing Grace

Words by John Newton
Traditional American Melody

First note

Moderately

1. A - maz - ing ___ grace, how sweet the sound that
2. 'Twas grace that ___ taught my heart to fear, and
3. The Lord has ___ prom - ised good to me, His
4., 5. *(See additional lyrics)*

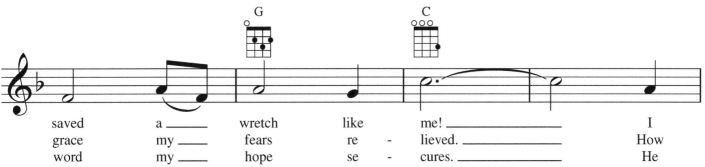

saved a _____ wretch like me! _____ I
grace my ____ fears re - lieved. _____ How
word my ____ hope se - cures. _____ He

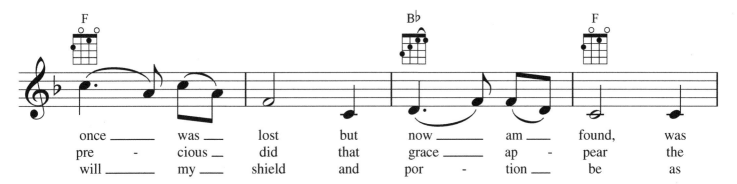

once _____ was ____ lost but now _____ am ____ found, was
pre - cious ____ did that grace _____ ap - pear the
will _____ my ____ shield and por - tion ____ be as

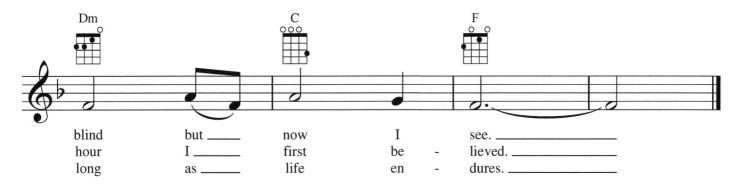

blind but ____ now I see. _____
hour I _____ first be - lieved. _____
long as _____ life en - dures. _____

Additional Lyrics

4. Through many dangers, toils and snares,
   I have already come.
   'Tis grace hath brought me safe thus far,
   And grace will lead me home.

5. When we've been there ten thousand years,
   Bright shining as the sun,
   We've no less days to sing God's praise
   Than when we'd first begun.

Beautiful Brown Eyes

Traditional

First note

Gently
Verse

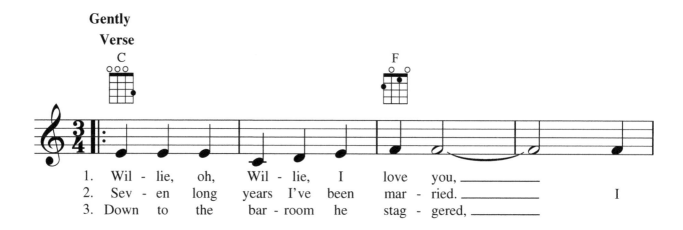

1. Wil - lie, oh, Wil - lie, I love you, _____
2. Sev - en long years I've been mar - ried. _____ I
3. Down to the bar - room he stag - gered, _____

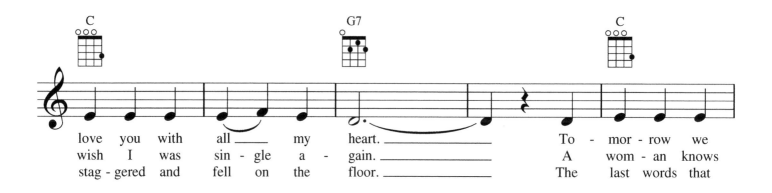

love you with all ___ my heart. _____ To - mor - row we
wish I was sin - gle a - gain. _____ A wom - an knows
stag - gered and fell on the floor. _____ The last words that

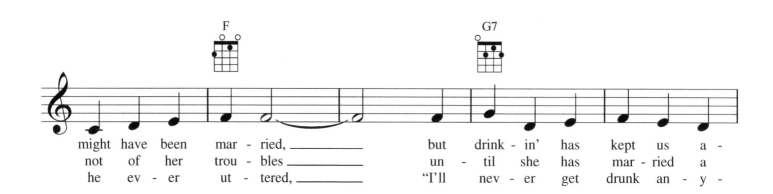

might have been mar - ried, _____ but drink - in' has kept us a -
not of her trou - bles _____ un - til she has mar - ried a
he ev - er ut - tered, _____ "I'll nev - er get drunk an - y -

Chorus

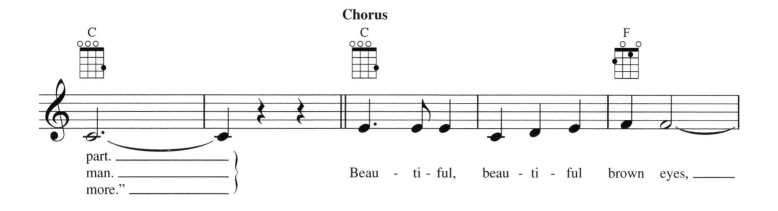

part. _____
man. _____
more." _____

Beau - ti - ful, beau - ti - ful brown eyes, _____

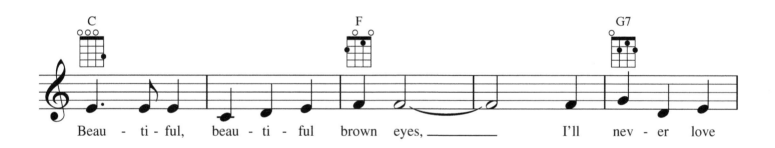

_____ beau - ti - ful, beau - ti - ful brown eyes. _____

Beau - ti - ful, beau - ti - ful brown eyes, _____ I'll nev - er love

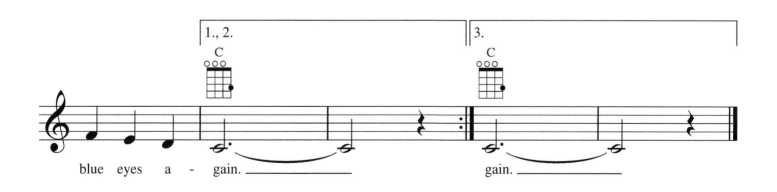

1., 2.
blue eyes a - gain. _____

3.
gain. _____

The Blue Tail Fly
(Jimmy Crack Corn)
Words and Music by Daniel Decatur Emmett

First note

Lively
Verse

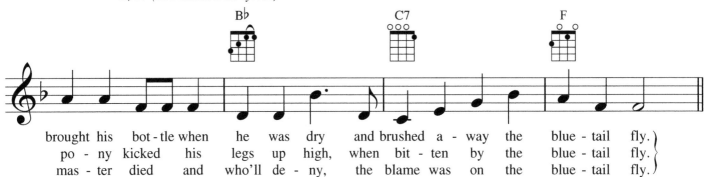

1. When I was young, I used to wait on mas-ter, hand-ing him his plate. I
2. He used to ride each af-ter-noon, I'd fol-low with a hick-'ry broom. The
3. The po-ny jump, he run, he pitch, he threw my mas-ter in the ditch. My

4., 5. *(See additional lyrics)*

brought his bot-tle when he was dry and brushed a-way the blue-tail fly.
po-ny kicked his legs up high, when bit-ten by the blue-tail fly.
mas-ter died and who'll de-ny, the blame was on the blue-tail fly.

Chorus

Jim-my crack corn and I don't care, Jim-my crack corn and I don't care,

Jim-my crack corn and I don't care, old mas-ter's gone a-way.

Additional Lyrics

4. Old master's dead and gone to rest,
   They say it happened for the best.
   I won't forget until I die
   My master and the blue-tail fly.
   Chorus

5. A skeeter bites right through your clothes,
   A hornet strikes you on the nose,
   The bees may get you passing by,
   But, oh, much worse, the blue-tail fly.
   Chorus

Buffalo Gals
(Won't You Come Out Tonight?)

Words and Music by Cool White (John Hodges)

Bury Me Not on the Lone Prairie

Words based on the poem "The Ocean Burial" by Rev. Edwin H. Chapin
Music by Ossian N. Dodge

First note

Mournfully

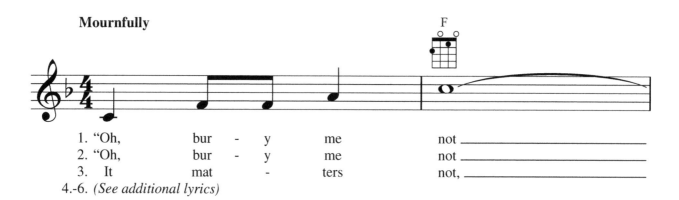

1. "Oh,   bur - y   me   not _____
2. "Oh,   bur - y   me   not _____
3. It   mat - ters   not, _____
4.-6. *(See additional lyrics)*

_____   on   the   lone   prai - rie." _____
_____   on   the   lone   prai - rie, _____
_____   I've _____   oft   been   told, _____

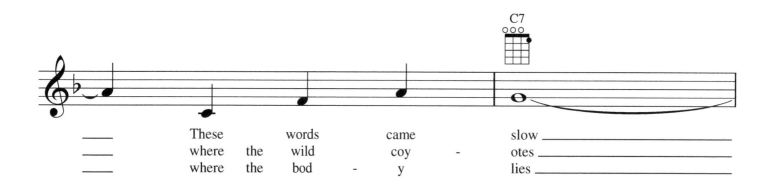

_____   These   words   came   slow _____
_____   where   the   wild   coy - otes _____
_____   where   the   bod - y   lies _____

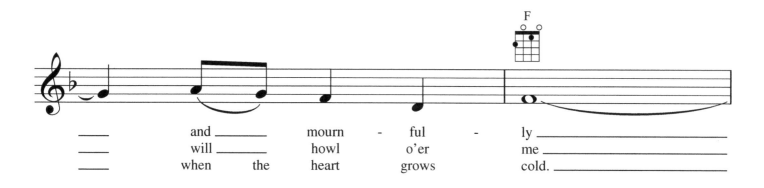

_____   and _____   mourn - ful - ly _____
_____   will _____   howl   o'er   me _____
_____   when   the   heart   grows   cold. _____

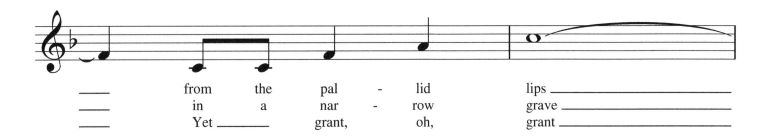

_____ from the pal - lid lips _____
_____ in a nar - row grave _____
_____ Yet _____ grant, oh, grant _____

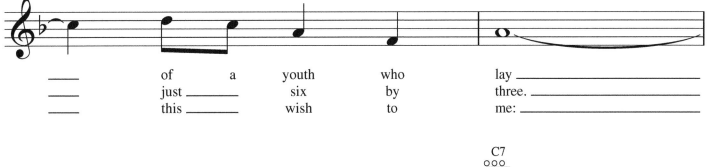

_____ of a youth who lay _____
_____ just _____ six by three. _____
_____ this _____ wish to me: _____

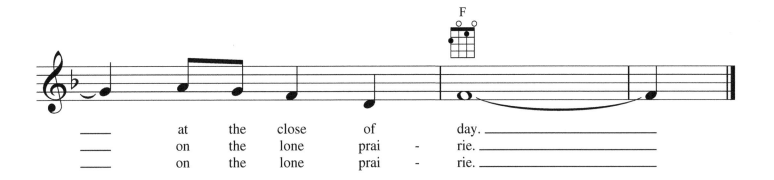

C7

_____ on his dy - ing bed _____
_____ Oh, _____ bur - y me not _____
_____ Oh, _____ bur - y me not _____

F

_____ at the close of day. _____
_____ on the lone prai - rie. _____
_____ on the lone prai - rie. _____

Additional Lyrics

4. I've always wished to be laid when I died
   In the little churchyard on the green hillside.
   By my father's grave there let mine be,
   And bury me not on the lone prairie."

5. "Oh, bury me not," and his voice failed there,
   But we took no heed of his dying prayer.
   In a narrow grave just six by three,
   We buried him there on the lone prairie.

6. And the cowboys now as they roam the plain,
   For they marked the spot where his bones were lain,
   Fling a handful of roses o'er his grave,
   With a prayer to Him who his soul will save.

Camptown Races

Words and Music by Stephen C. Foster

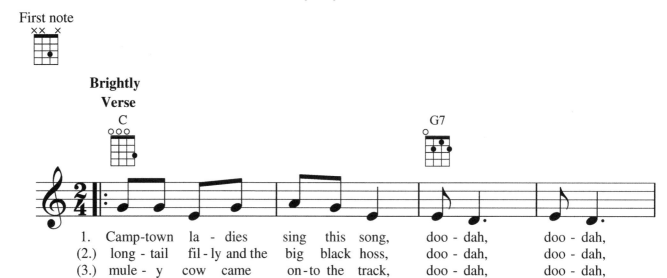

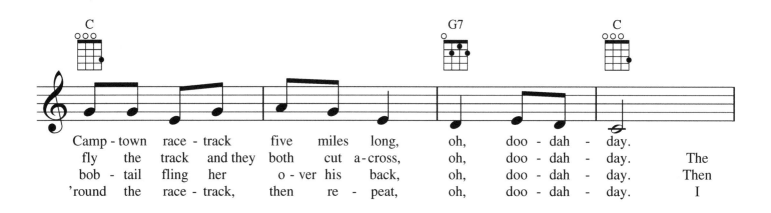

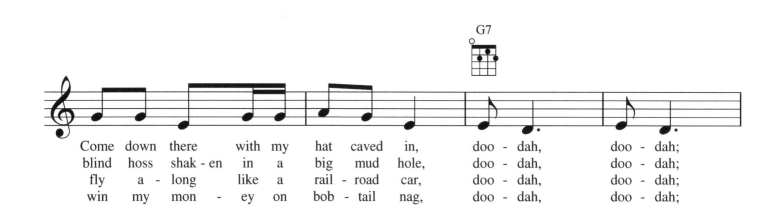

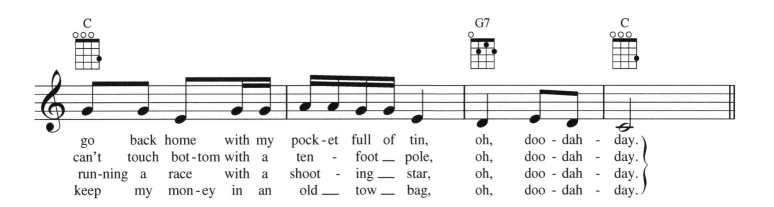

go back home with my pock-et full of tin, oh, doo - dah - day.
can't touch bot-tom with a ten - foot __ pole, oh, doo - dah - day.
run-ning a race with a shoot - ing __ star, oh, doo - dah - day.
keep my mon-ey in an old __ tow __ bag, oh, doo-dah - day.

Chorus

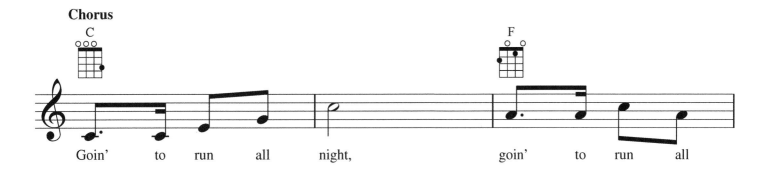

Goin' to run all night, goin' to run all

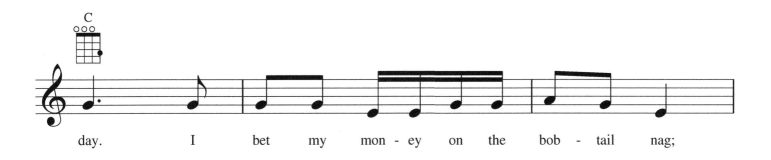

day. I bet my mon - ey on the bob - tail nag;

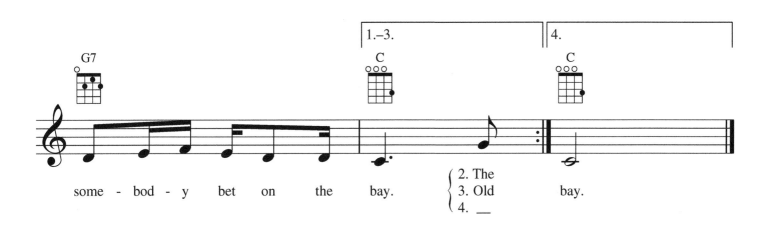

| 1.–3. | 4. |

some - bod - y bet on the bay.

2. The
3. Old bay.
4. __

Careless Love

Anonymous

First note

Slowly

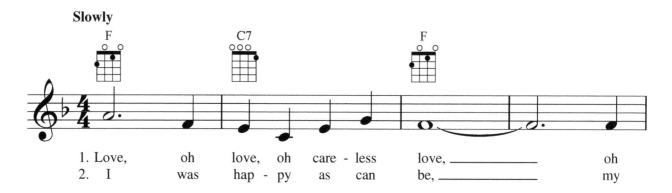

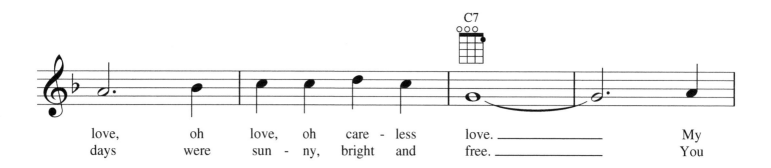

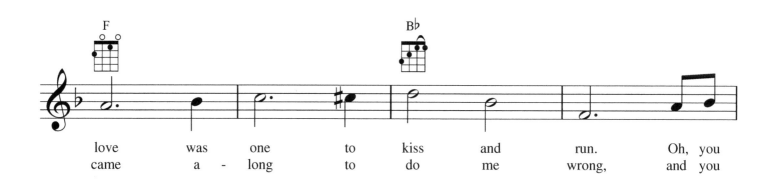

(Oh, My Darling)
Clementine

Words and Music by Percy Montrose

Carry Me Back to Old Virginny

Words and Music by James A. Bland

First note

Gently

1. Car - ry me back to old Vir - gin - ny,
2. Car - ry me back to old Vir - gin - ny,

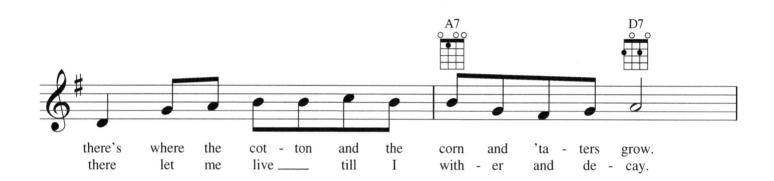

there's where the cot - ton and the corn and 'ta - ters grow.
there let me live _____ till I with - er and de - cay.

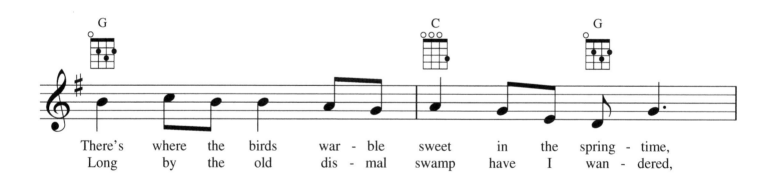

There's where the birds war - ble sweet in the spring - time,
Long by the old dis - mal swamp have I wan - dered,

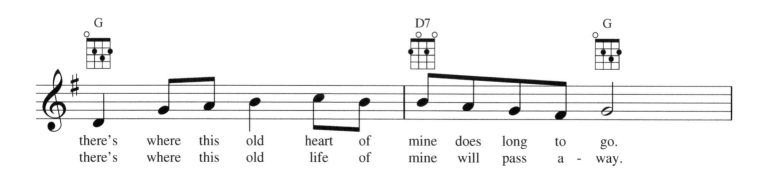

there's where this old heart of mine does long to go.
there's where this old life of mine will pass a - way.

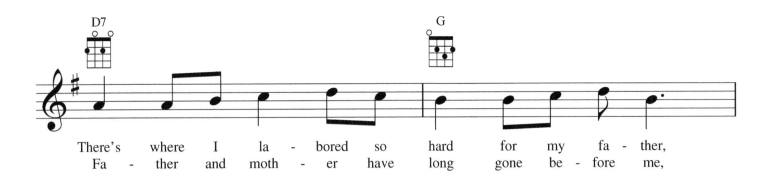

There's where I la - bored so hard for my fa - ther,
Fa - ther and moth - er have long gone be - fore me,

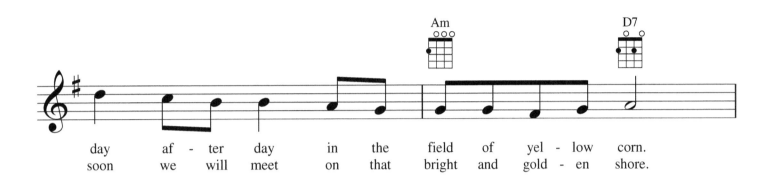

day af - ter day in the field of yel - low corn.
soon we will meet on that bright and gold - en shore.

No place on earth do I love more sin - cere - ly
There we'll be hap - py and free from all sor - row,

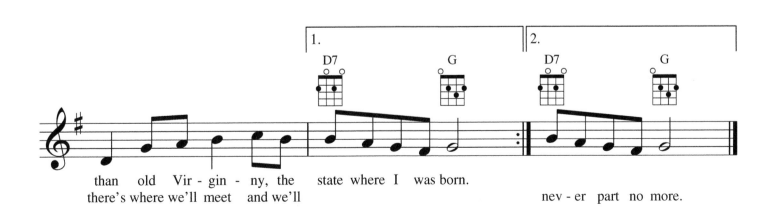

1.
than old Vir - gin - ny, the state where I was born.
there's where we'll meet and we'll

2.
nev - er part no more.

The Crawdad Song

Traditional

First note

Moderately, in 2

1. You get a line and I'll get a pole, _____
2. Get up, old _____ man, you slept too _____ late, _____
3. Get up, old _____ wom - an, you slept too _____ late, _____

4., 5. *(See additional lyrics)*

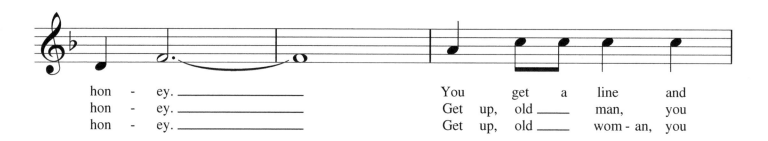

hon - ey. _____ You get a line and
hon - ey. _____ Get up, old _____ man, you
hon - ey. _____ Get up, old _____ wom - an, you

I'll get a pole, _____ babe. _____
slept too _____ late, _____ babe. _____
slept too _____ late, _____ babe. _____

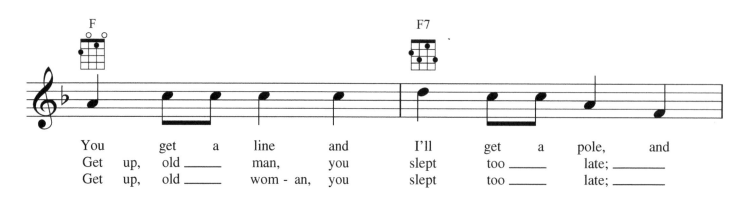

You get a line and I'll get a pole, and
Get up, old _____ man, you slept too _____ late; _____
Get up, old _____ wom - an, you slept too _____ late; _____

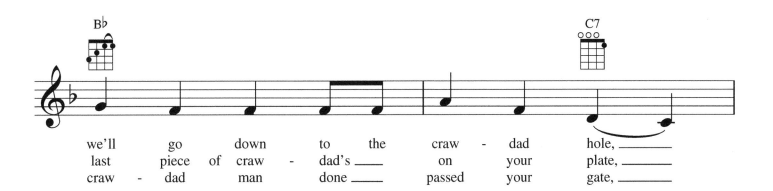

we'll	go	down	to the	craw - dad	hole, _____
last	piece of	craw -	dad's ___	on your	plate, _____
craw - dad	man	done ___	passed your	gate, _____

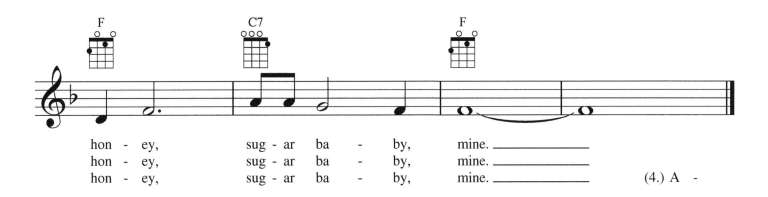

hon - ey,	sug - ar ba - by,	mine. _____
hon - ey,	sug - ar ba - by,	mine. _____
hon - ey,	sug - ar ba - by,	mine. _____ (4.) A -

Additional Lyrics

4. Along come a man with a sack on his back, honey.
   Along come a man with a sack on his back, babe.
   Along come a man with a sack on his back,
   Packin' all the crawdads he can pack, honey, sugar baby, mine.

5. What you gonna do when the lake goes dry, honey?
   What you gonna do when the lake goes dry, babe?
   What you gonna do when the lake goes dry?
   Sit on the bank and watch the crawdads die, honey, sugar baby, mine.

Down by the Riverside

African-American Spiritual

First note

Rhythmically
Verse

1. Gon-na   lay down   my   bur - den ___
(2.) lay down   my   sword   and shield } down   by   the
(3.) try   on   my   long   white robe

riv - er - side, ___   down by   the   riv - er - side, ___

down by   the   riv - er - side. ___ { Gon - na   lay down   my
Gon - na   lay down   my
Gon - na   try   on   my

bur - den ___ }
sword   and shield } down   by   the   riv - er - side ___   and
long   white robe

stud - y _____   war   no   more.

Chorus

I ain't gon - na stud - y war ___ no more. Ain't gon - na

stud - y war ___ no more. Ain't gon - na stud - y

war no more. I ain't gon - na

stud - y war ___ no more. Ain't gon - na stud - y war ___ no

more. Ain't gon - na stud - y _____ war no

1., 2.   **3.**

more. _____ { 2. Gon - na   more. _____
                { 3. Gon - na

Down in the Valley

Traditional American Folksong

Dry Bones

Traditional

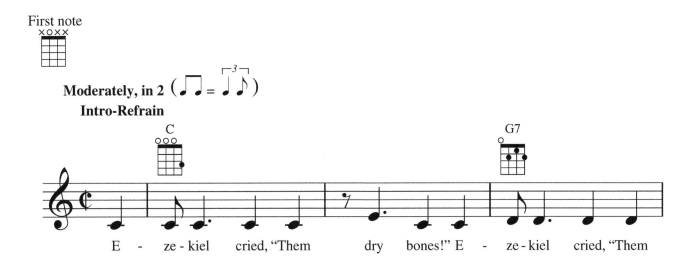

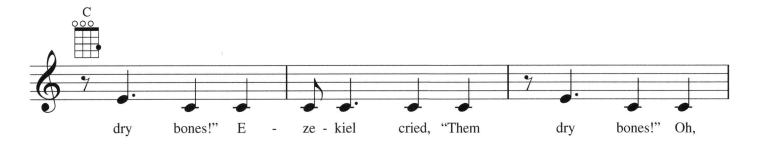

E - ze - kiel cried, "Them dry bones!" E - ze - kiel cried, "Them

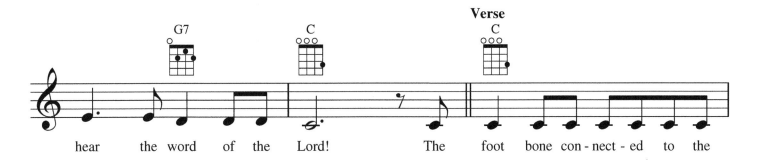

dry bones!" E - ze - kiel cried, "Them dry bones!" Oh,

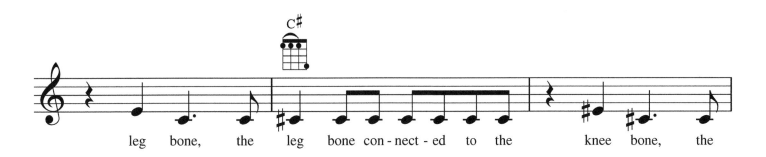

hear the word of the Lord! The foot bone con - nect - ed to the

leg bone, the leg bone con - nect - ed to the knee bone, the

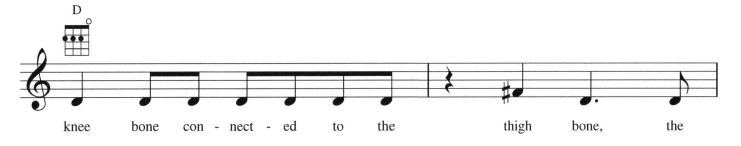

knee bone con - nect - ed to the thigh bone, the

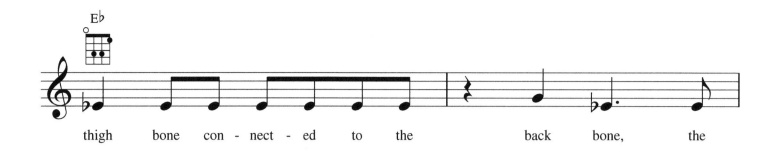

thigh bone con - nect - ed to the back bone, the

back bone con - nect - ed to the neck bone, the

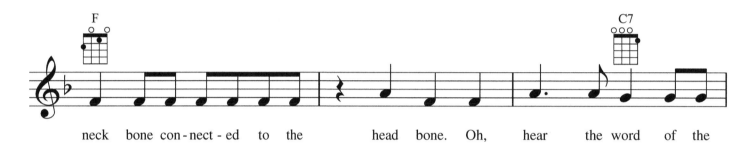

neck bone con - nect - ed to the head bone. Oh, hear the word of the

Refrain

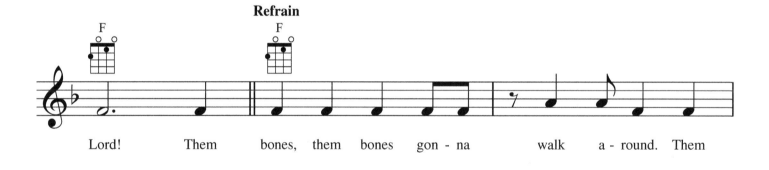

Lord! Them bones, them bones gon - na walk a - round. Them

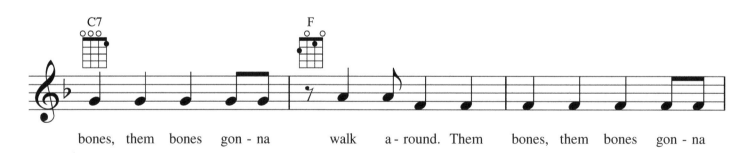

bones, them bones gon - na walk a - round. Them bones, them bones gon - na

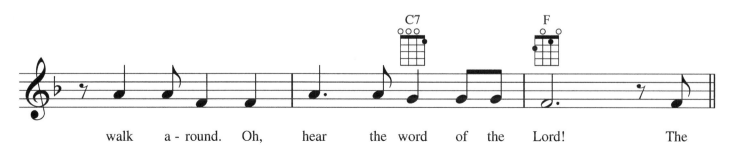

walk a - round. Oh, hear the word of the Lord! The

Verse

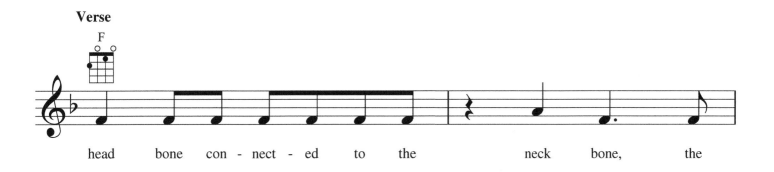

head   bone   con - nect - ed   to   the   neck   bone,   the

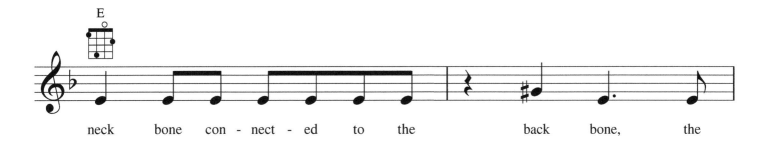

neck   bone   con - nect - ed   to   the   back   bone,   the

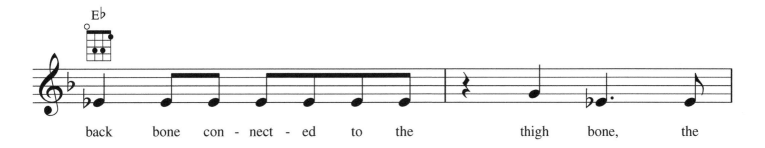

back   bone   con - nect - ed   to   the   thigh   bone,   the

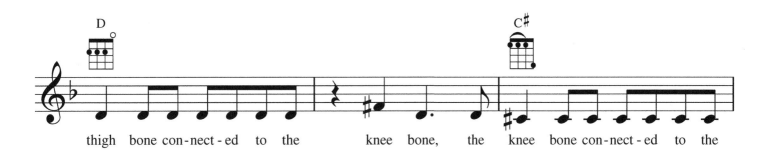

thigh   bone con - nect - ed   to   the   knee   bone,   the   knee   bone con - nect - ed   to   the

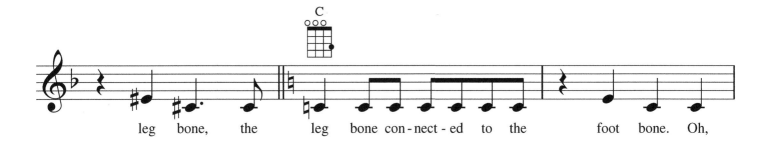

leg   bone,   the   leg   bone con - nect - ed   to   the   foot   bone.   Oh,

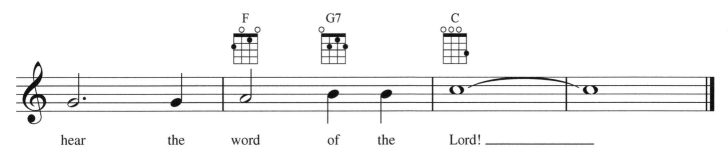

hear   the   word   of   the   Lord! _____

For He's a Jolly Good Fellow

Traditional

First note

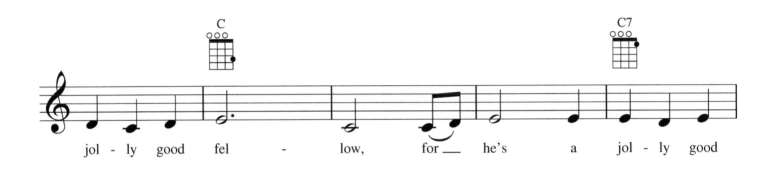

For he's a jol - ly good fel - low, for he's a

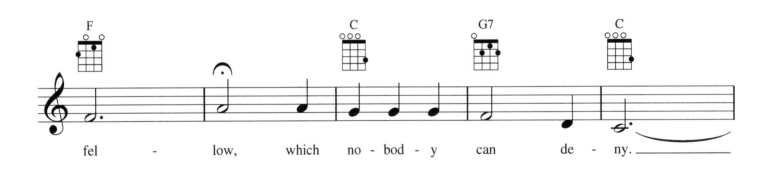

jol - ly good fel - low, for ___ he's a jol - ly good

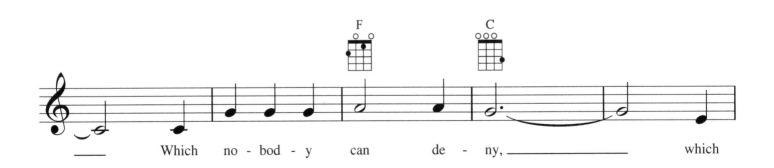

fel - low, which no - bod - y can de - ny. ___

___ Which no - bod - y can de - ny, _____ which

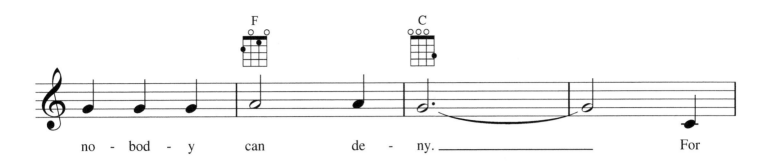

no - bod - y   can   de - ny. _____   For

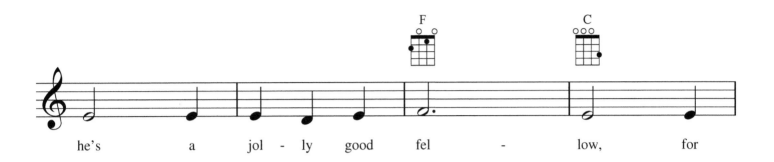

he's   a   jol - ly   good   fel   -   low,   for

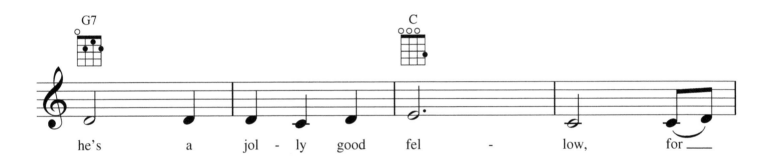

he's   a   jol - ly   good   fel   -   low,   for ____

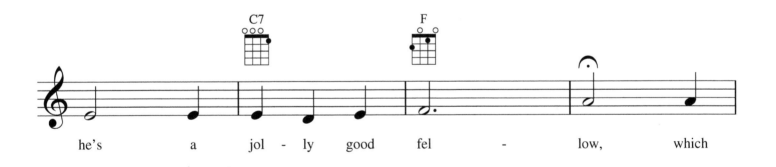

he's   a   jol - ly   good   fel   -   low,   which

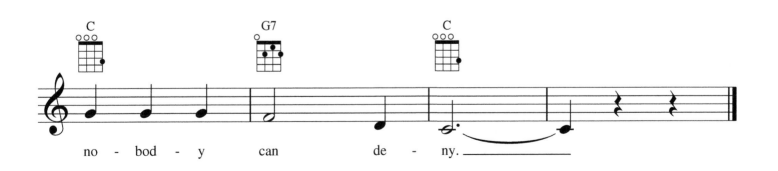

no - bod - y   can   de - ny. _____

Freight Train

Words and Music by Elizabeth Cotten

First note

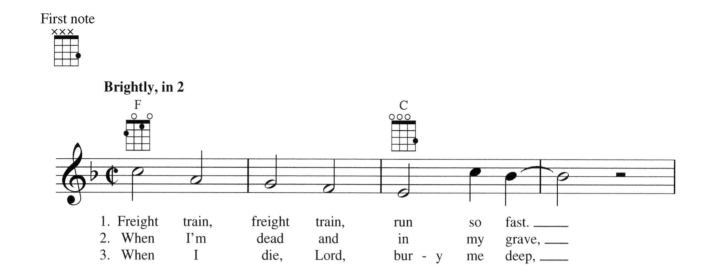

Brightly, in 2

1. Freight train, freight train, run so fast. ____
2. When I'm dead and in my grave, ____
3. When I die, Lord, bur - y me deep, ____

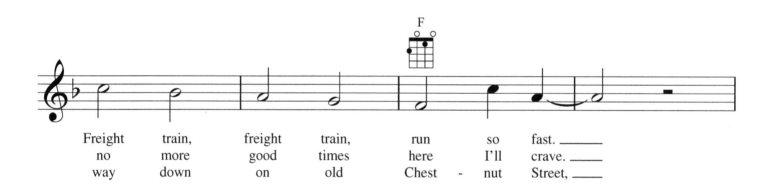

Freight train, freight train, run so fast. ____
no more freight good times here I'll crave. ____
way down on old Chest - nut Street, ____

Please don't tell what ___ train I'm on; ___ they won't
Place the stones at my head and feet, and tell them
so I can hear old Num - ber Nine ___ as ___

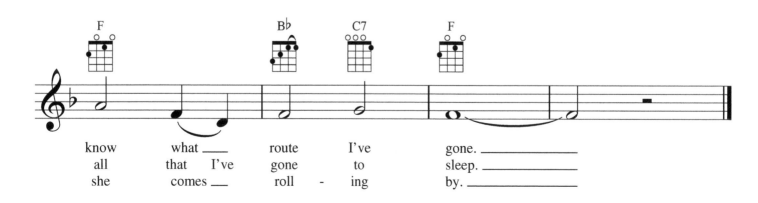

know what ___ route I've gone. _____
all that I've gone to sleep. _____
she comes ___ roll - ing by. _____

Give Me That Old Time Religion

Traditional

Go Tell Aunt Rhody

Traditional

First note

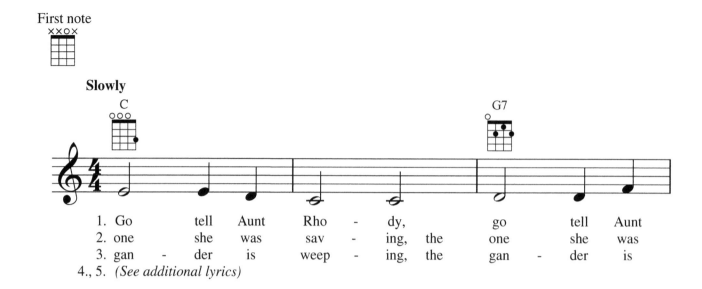

Slowly

1. Go tell Aunt Rho - dy, go tell Aunt
2. one she was sav - ing, the one she was
3. gan - der is weep - ing, the gan - der is

4., 5. *(See additional lyrics)*

Rho - dy, go tell Aunt Rho - dy the
sav - ing, the one she was sav - ing to
weep - ing, the gan - der is weep - ing be -

1.–4.

5.

old grey goose is dead. The head.
make a feath - er bed. The
cause his wife is dead. The

Additional Lyrics

4. The goslings are crying, *(3 times)*
Because their mama's dead.

5. She died in the water, *(3 times)*
With her heels above her head.

Go, Tell It on the Mountain

African-American Spiritual
Verses by John W. Work, Jr.

Good Night Ladies

Words by E.P. Christy
Traditional Music

First note

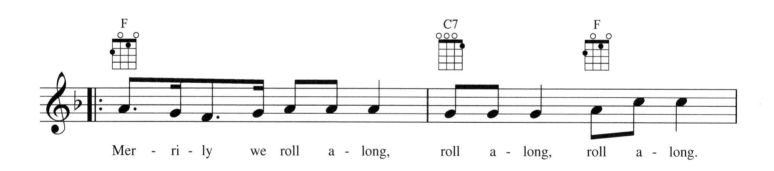

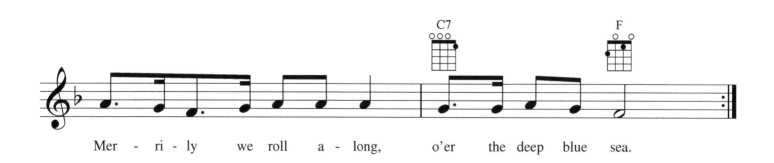

Hail, Hail, The Gang's All Here

Words by D.A. Esrom
Music by Theodore F. Morse and Arthur Sullivan

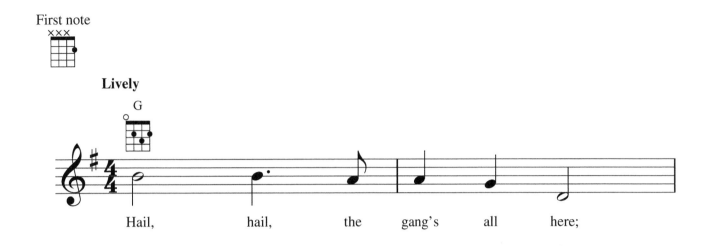

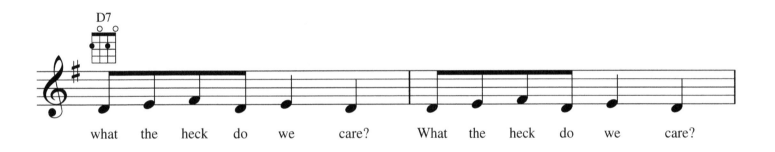

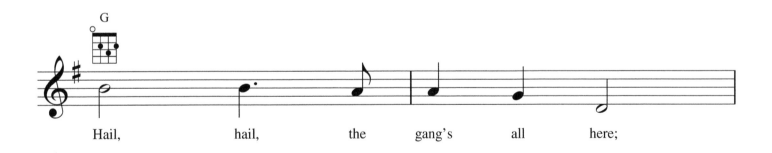

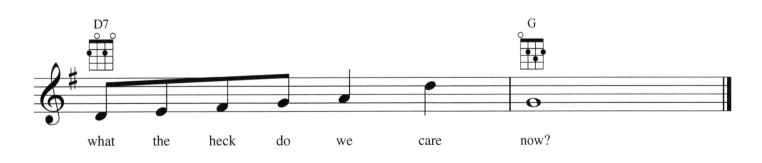

He's Got the Whole World in His Hands

Traditional Spiritual

First note

Moderately

He's got the whole world _ in His hands. _ He's got the

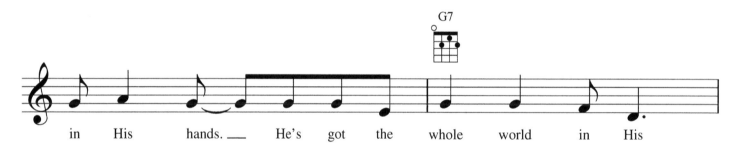

whole world _ in His hands. _ He's got the whole world _

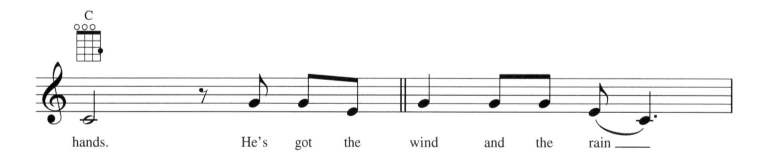

in His hands. __ He's got the whole world in His

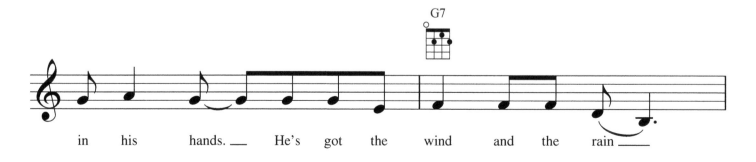

hands. He's got the wind and the rain _____

in his hands. __ He's got the wind and the rain _____

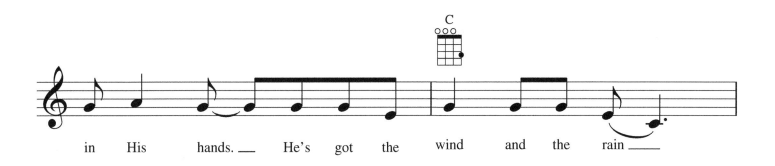

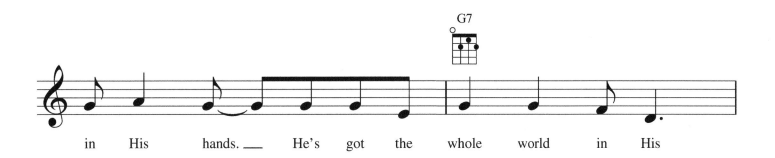

in His hands. ___ He's got the wind and the rain ___

in His hands. ___ He's got the whole world in His

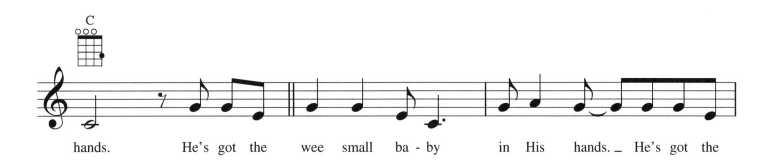

hands. He's got the wee small ba - by in His hands. ___ He's got the

wee small ba - by in his hands. ___ Oh, He's got ev - 'ry - bod - y

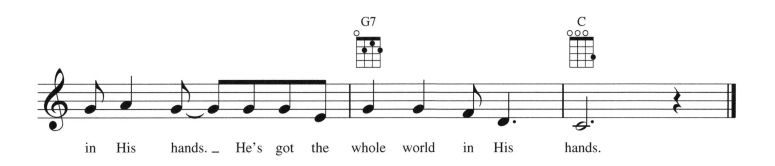

in His hands. ___ He's got the whole world in His hands.

Home on the Range

Lyrics by Dr. Brewster Higley
Music by Dan Kelly

First note

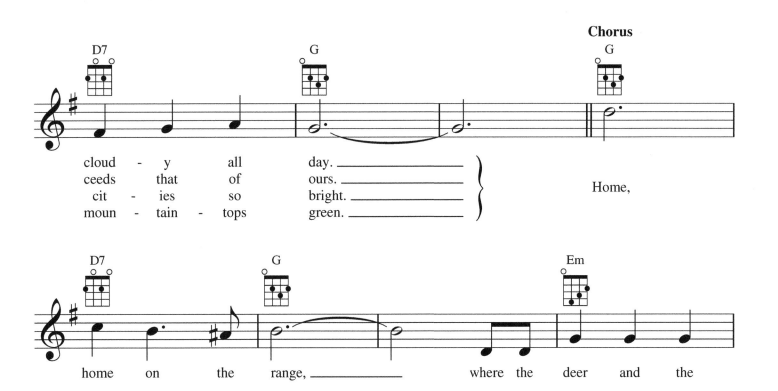

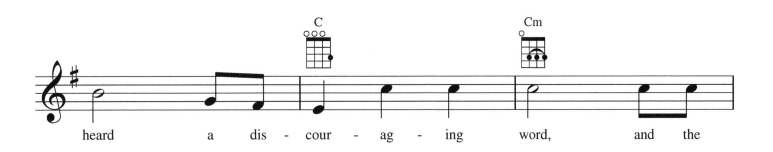

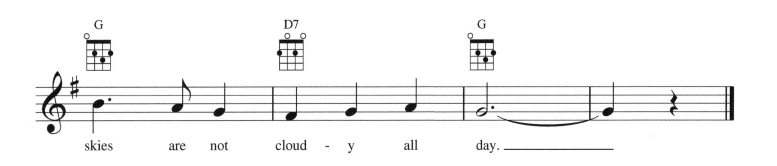

Home Sweet Home

Words by John Howard Payne
Music by Henry R. Bishop

First note

Gently
Verse

1. 'Mid _____ pleas - ures and pal - ac - es
(2.) ex - ile from home, splen - dor
(3.) thee, I'll re - turn, o - ver -

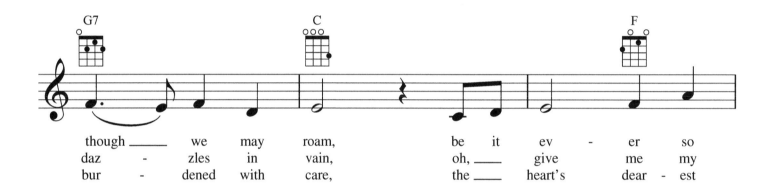

though _____ we may roam, be it ev - er so
daz - zles in vain, oh, _____ give me my
bur - dened with care, the _____ heart's dear - est

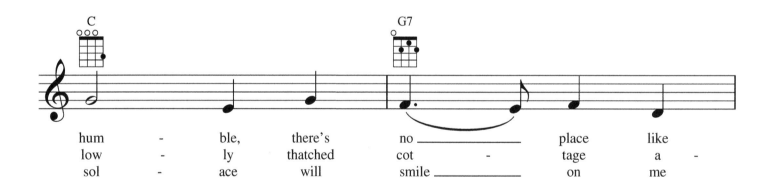

hum - ble, there's no _____ place like
low - ly thatched cot - tage a -
sol - ace will smile _____ on me

home. A charm _____ from the sky seems to
gain. The birds _____ sing - ing gai - ly, that
there. No more _____ from that cot - tage a -

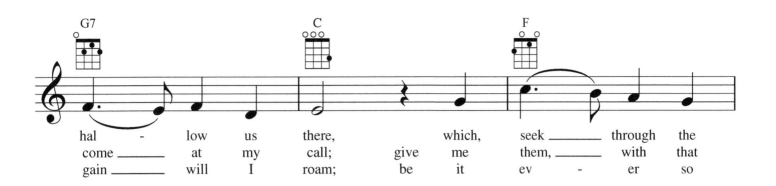

hal - low us there, which, seek _____ through the
come _____ at my call; give me them, _____ with that
gain _____ will I roam; be it ev - er so

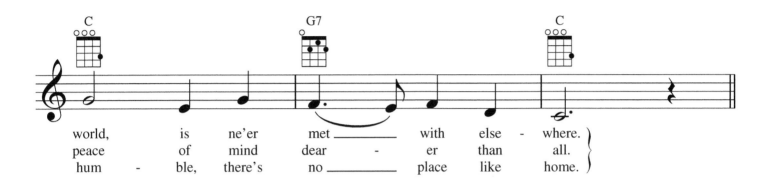

world, is ne'er met _____ with else - where.
peace of mind dear - er than all.
hum - ble, there's no _____ place like home.

Chorus

Home! Home! Sweet home. _____ There's no _____ place like

home. Home! Home! Sweet home. _____ There's

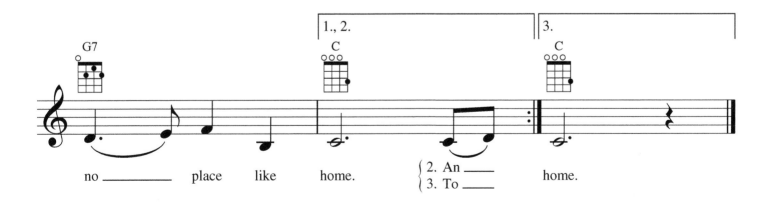

no _____ place like home.

1., 2.
3.

{ 2. An _____ home.
{ 3. To _____

I Wish I Was Single Again

Words and Music by J.C. Beckel

First note

1. I wish I was sin - gle, oh then, oh then, __ I
2. I mar - ried a wife, __ oh then, oh then, __ I
3. My wife __ took sick, __ oh then, oh then, __ my

4.-7. *(See additional lyrics)*

wish I was sin - gle, oh then. _____ When I was sin - gle, my
mar - ried a wife, __ oh then. _____ I mar - ried a wife, she's the
wife __ took sick, __ oh then. _____ My wife took sick, I went for the

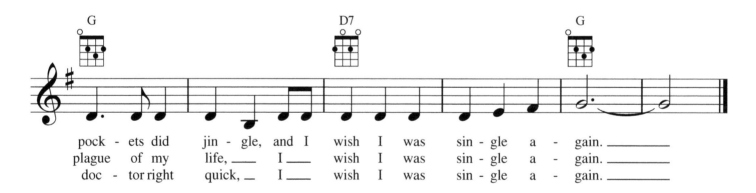

pock - ets did jin - gle, and I wish I was sin - gle a - gain. _____
plague of my life, __ I __ wish I was sin - gle a - gain. _____
doc - tor right quick, __ I __ wish I was sin - gle a - gain. _____

Additional Lyrics

4. My wife, she died, oh then, oh then,
   My wife, she died, oh then.
   My wife, she died, dang little cared I,
   To think I was single again.

5. I married another, oh then, oh then,
   I married another, oh then.
   I married another, she's the devil's stepmother,
   And I wish I was single again.

6. She beat me, she banged me, oh then, oh then,
   She beat me, she banged me, oh then.
   She beat me, she banged me, she swore she would hang me,
   I wish I was single again.

7. She got the rope, oh then, oh then,
   She got the rope, oh then.
   She got the rope and she greased it with soap,
   And I wish I was single again.

In the Good Old Summertime

Words by Ren Shields
Music by George Evans

you are in clo - ver and life is one beau - ti - ful
now fond - ly treas - ure, when we nev - er thought it a

rhyme. _____ No trou - ble an - noy - ing, each
crime _____ to go steal - ing cher - ries with

one is en - joy - ing the good old sum - mer -
face brown as ber - ries, _____ good old sum - mer

Refrain

time. _____
time. _____ In the good old sum - mer -

time, _____ in the good old sum - mer -

time, _____ stroll - ing through the

shad - y lanes with your ba - by mine. _____ You hold her hand and she holds yours, and that's a ver - y good sign _____ that she's your toot - sey woot - sey in the good old sum - mer - time. _____ 2. To time. _____

I've Been Working on the Railroad

American Folksong

John Brown's Body

Traditional

First note

March-like
Verse

1. John Brown's _ bod - y lies a - moul - d'ring in the grave,
2. The stars of heav - en are look - ing kind - ly down,
3. gone to be a sol - dier in the ar - my of the Lord, he's
4.-7. *(See additional lyrics)*

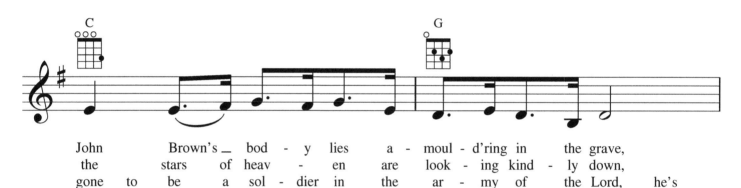

John Brown's _ bod - y lies a - moul - d'ring in the grave,
the stars of heav - en are look - ing kind - ly down,
gone to be a sol - dier in the ar - my of the Lord, he's

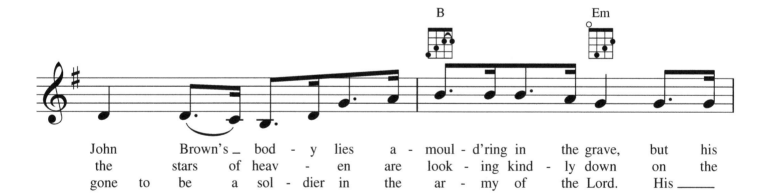

John Brown's _ bod - y lies a - moul - d'ring in the grave, but his
the stars of heav - en are look - ing kind - ly down on the
gone to be a sol - dier in the ar - my of the Lord. His _

Refrain

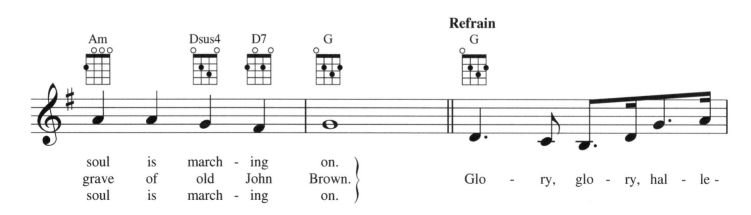

soul is march - ing on.
grave of old John Brown.   Glo - ry, glo - ry, hal - le -
soul is march - ing on.

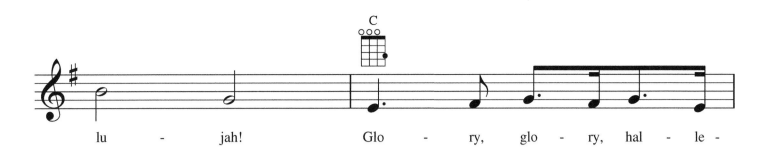

lu - jah! Glo - ry, glo - ry, hal - le -

lu - jah! glo - ry, glo - ry, hal - le - lu - jah! His

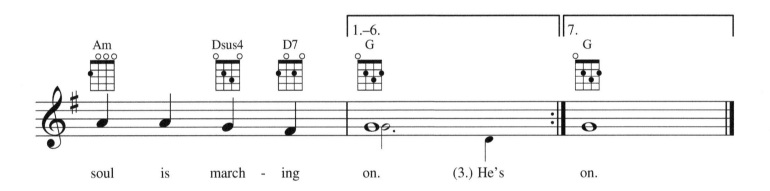

soul is march - ing on. (3.) He's on.

Additional Lyrics

4. John Brown died that the slave might be free,
   John Brown died that the slave might be free,
   John Brown died that the slave might be free,
   But his soul goes marching on.

5. John Brown's knapsack is strapped to his back,
   John Brown's knapsack is strapped to his back,
   John Brown's knapsack is strapped to his back.
   His soul is marching on.

6. His pet lambs will meet on the way,
   His pet lambs will meet on the way,
   His pet lambs will meet on the way,
   And they'll go marching on.

7. They will hang Jeff Davis on a sour apple tree,
   They will hang Jeff Davis on a sour apple tree,
   They will hang Jeff Davis on a sour apple tree
   As they go marching on.

Kumbaya

Congo Folksong

First note

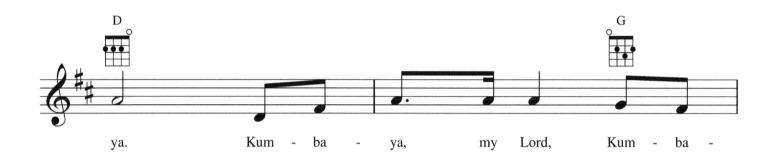

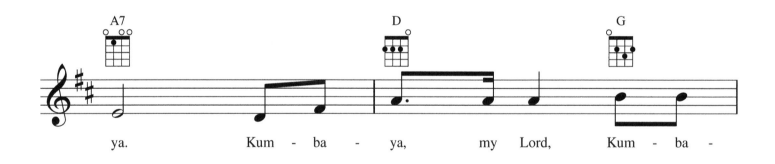

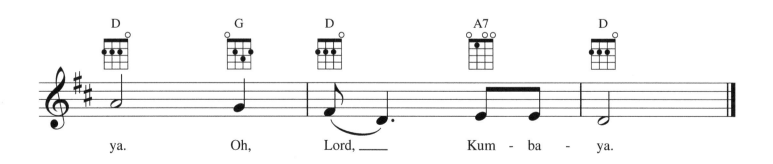

Lavender's Blue

English Folksong

Little Brown Jug

Words and Music by Joseph E. Winner

Mama Don't 'Low

American Folksong

First note

Brightly

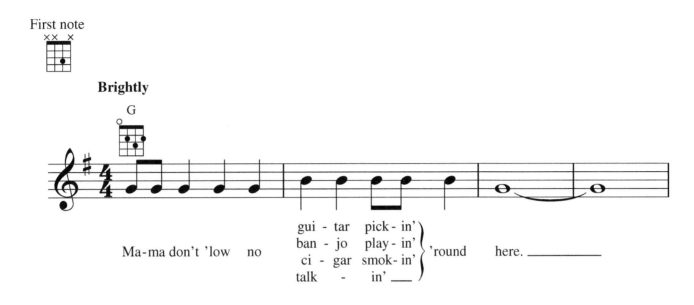

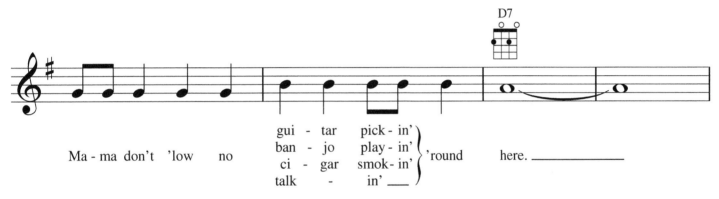

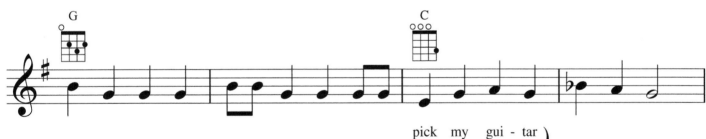

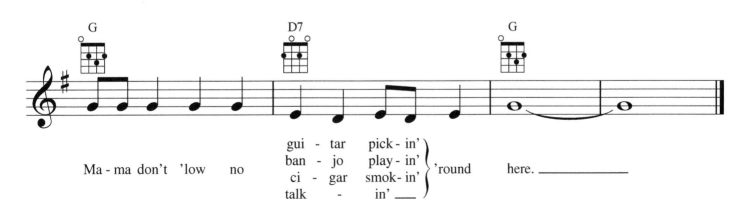

Marianne

Traditional

First note

Moderately, in 2
Verse

1. Mar - i - anne, oh, Mar - i - anne, oh,
2. When I met sweet Mar - i - anne, her

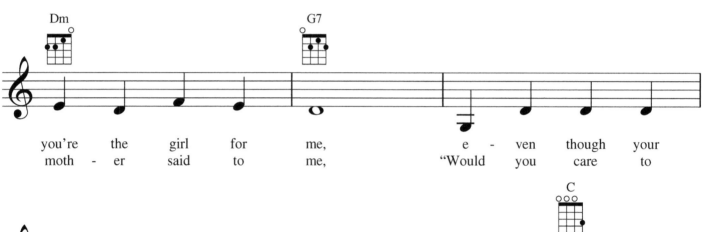

you're the girl for me, e - ven though your
moth - er said to me, "Would you though care to

dear old ma - ma will not say "Si, si."
tell me where you will stand fi - nan - cial - ly?"

Mar - i - anne, oh, Mar - i - anne, oh,
She dos not ap - prove of me 'cause

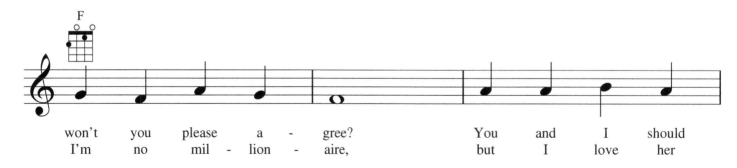

won't you please a - gree? You and I should
I'm no mil - lion - aire, but I love her

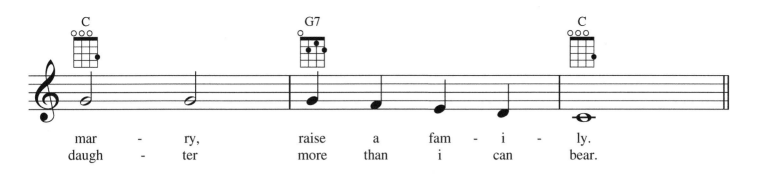

mar - ry, raise a fam - i - ly.
daugh - ter more than i can bear.

Refrain

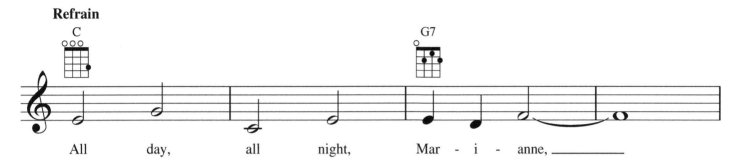

All day, all night, Mar - i - anne, _____

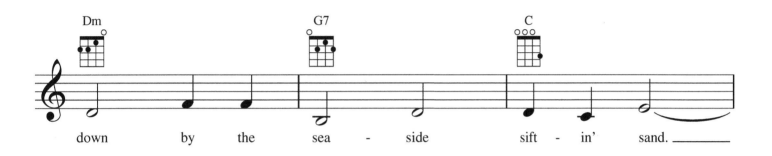

down by the sea - side sift - in' sand. _____

_____ All the lit - tle chil - dren love

Mar - i - anne, _____ down by the

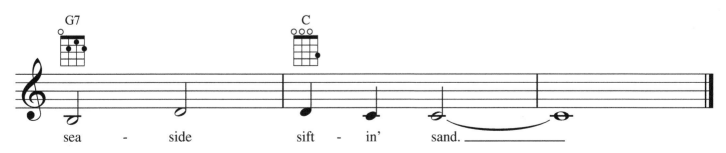

sea - side sift - in' sand. _____

Michael, Row the Boat Ashore

Traditional Folksong

First note

Moderately, in 2

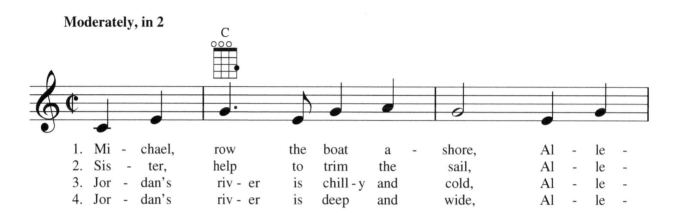

1. Mi - chael, row the boat a - shore, Al - le -
2. Sis - ter, help to trim the sail, Al - le -
3. Jor - dan's riv - er is chill - y and cold, Al - le -
4. Jor - dan's riv - er is deep and wide, Al - le -

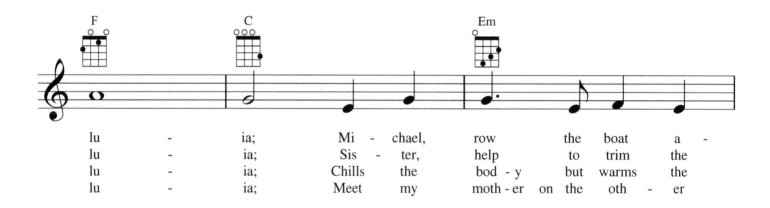

lu - ia; Mi - chael, row the boat a -
lu - ia; Sis - ter, help to trim the
lu - ia; Chills the bod - y but warms the
lu - ia; Meet my moth - er on the oth - er

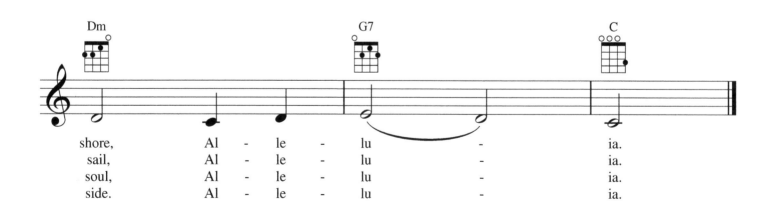

shore, Al - le - lu - ia.
sail, Al - le - lu - ia.
soul, Al - le - lu - ia.
side. Al - le - lu - ia.

My Bonnie Lies Over the Ocean

Traditional

Molly Malone
(Cockles & Mussels)

Irish Folksong

First note

Moderate Waltz
Verse

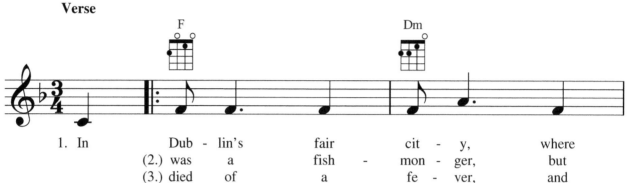

1. In Dub - lin's fair cit - y, where
(2.) was a fish - mon - ger, but
(3.) died of a fe - ver, and

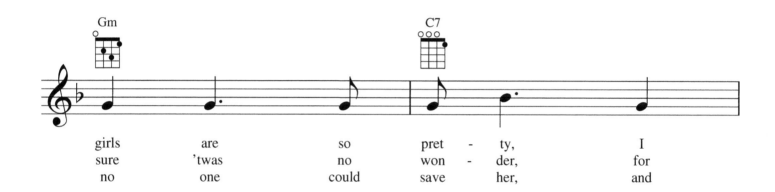

girls are so pret - ty, I
sure 'twas no won - der, for
no one could save her, and

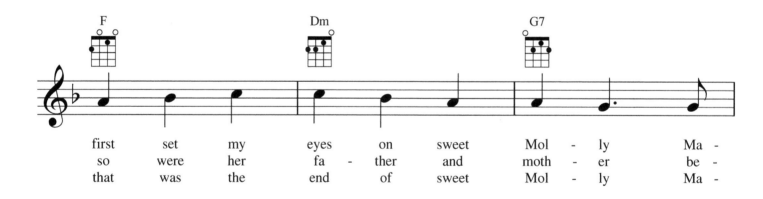

first set my eyes on sweet Mol - ly Ma -
so were her fa - ther and moth - er be -
that was the end of sweet Mol - ly Ma -

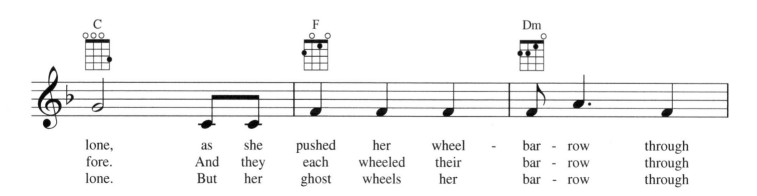

lone, as she pushed her wheel - bar - row through
fore. And they each wheeled their bar - row through
lone. But her ghost wheels her bar - row through

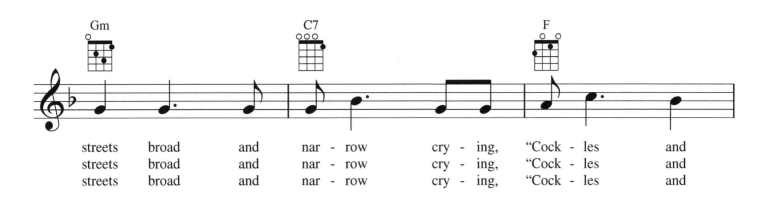

streets broad and nar - row cry - ing, "Cock - les and
streets broad and nar - row cry - ing, "Cock - les and
streets broad and nar - row cry - ing, "Cock - les and

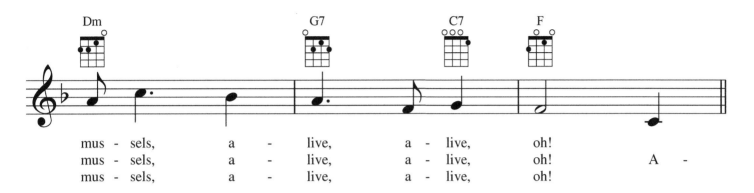

mus - sels, a - live, a - live, oh!
mus - sels, a - live, a - live, oh! A -
mus - sels, a - live, a - live, oh!

Refrain

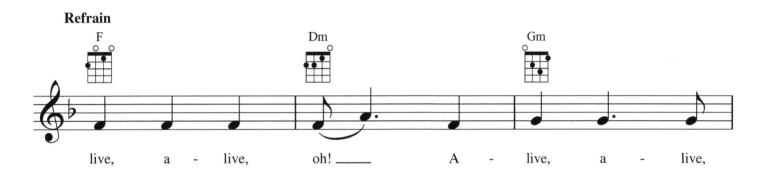

live, a - live, oh! _____ A - live, a - live,

oh!" ____ Cry - ing, "Cock - les and mus - sels, a -

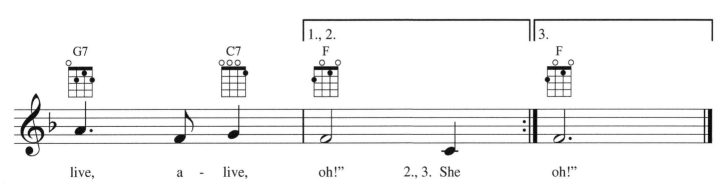

live, a - live, oh!" 2., 3. She   oh!"

57

My Wild Irish Rose

Words and Music by Chauncey Olcott

First note

Slowly, with much expression

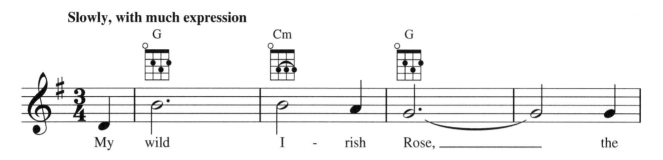

My wild I - rish Rose, _____ the

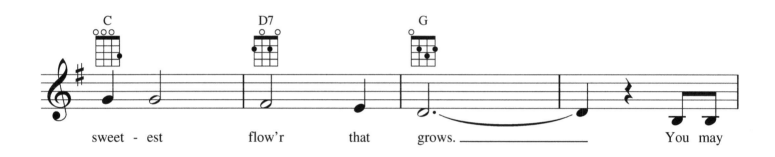

sweet - est flow'r that grows. _____ You may

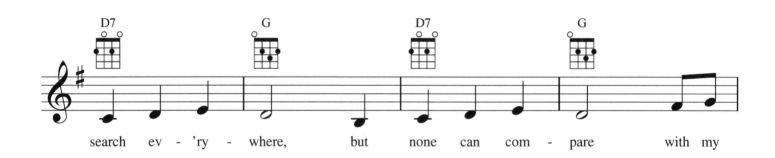

search ev - 'ry - where, but none can com - pare with my

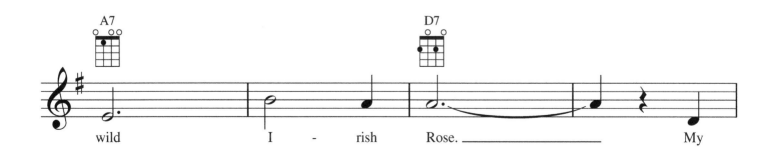

wild I - rish Rose. _____ My

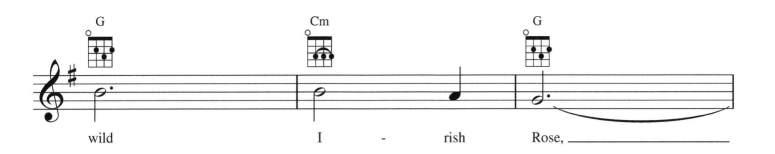

wild   I - rish   Rose, _____

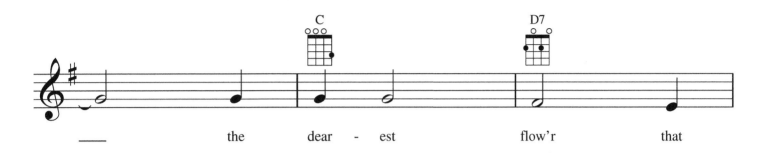

___   the   dear - est   flow'r   that

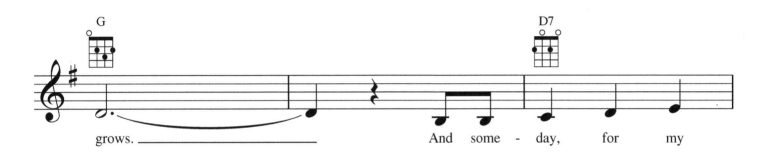

grows. _____   And   some - day,   for   my

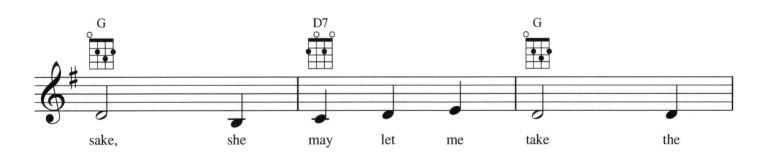

sake,   she   may   let   me   take   the

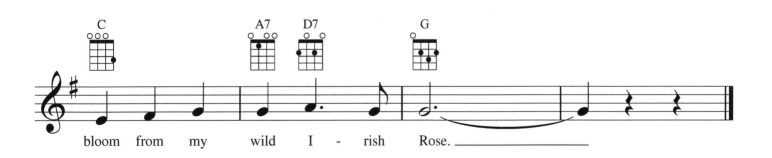

bloom   from   my   wild   I - rish   Rose. _____

Oh! Susanna

Words and Music by Stephen C. Foster

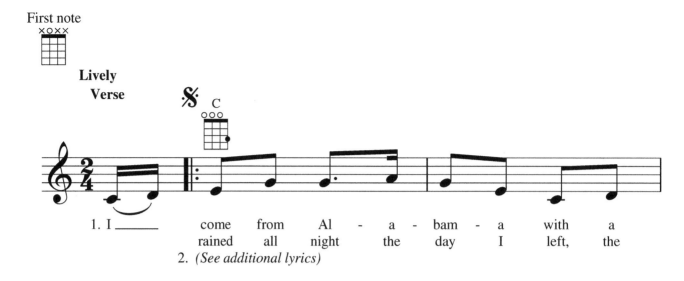

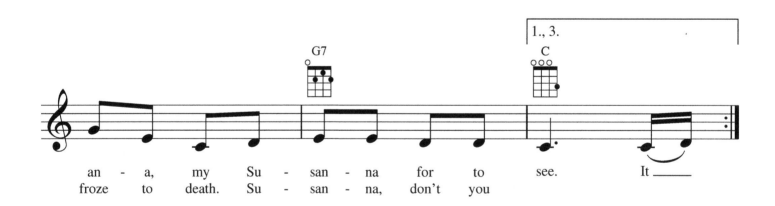

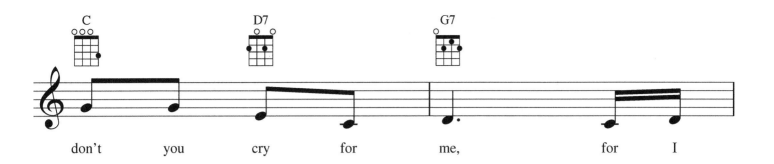

don't you cry for me, for I

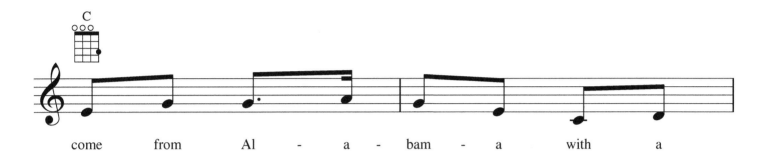

come from Al - a - bam - a with a

To Coda ⊕   **⊕ Coda**

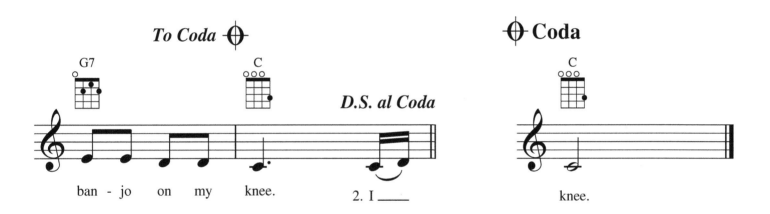

D.S. al Coda

ban - jo on my knee.   2. I ___   knee.

Additional Lyrics

2. I had a dream the other night
   When everything was still.
   I thought I saw Susanna
   A-coming down the hill.
   The buckwheat cake was in her mouth,
   The tear was in her eye,
   Say I, "I'm coming from the South.
   Susanna, don't you cry."
   Chorus

Oh Where, Oh Where Has My Little Dog Gone

Words by Sep. Winner
Traditional Melody

First note

Oh where, oh where has my lit - tle dog

gone? Oh where, oh where can he be? _____

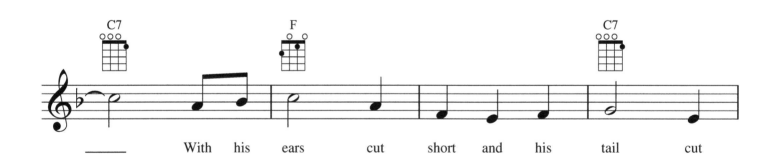

_____ With his ears cut short and his tail cut

long; oh where, oh where can he be? _____

On Top of Old Smoky

Kentucky Mountain Folksong

First note

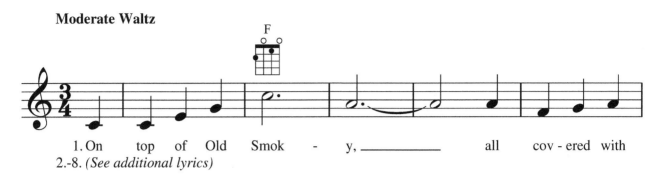

1. On top of Old Smok - y, _____ all cov - ered with
2.-8. *(See additional lyrics)*

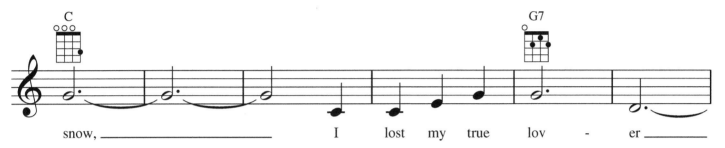

snow, _____ I lost my true lov - er _____

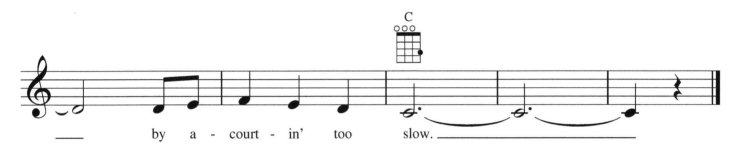

_____ by a - court - in' too slow. _____

Additional Lyrics

2. Well, a-courtin's a pleasure
   And parting is grief,
   But a false-hearted lover
   Is worse than a thief.

3. A thief, he will rob you
   And take all you have,
   But a false-hearted lover
   Will send you to your grave.

4. And the grave will decay you
   And turn you to dust.
   And where is the young man
   A poor girl can trust?

5. They'll hug you and kiss you
   And tell you more lies
   Than the cross-ties on the railroad
   Or the stars in the skies.

6. They'll tell you they love you
   Just to give your heart ease.
   but the minute your back's turned,
   They'll court whom they please.

7. So come, all you young maidens,
   And listen to me.
   Never place your affection
   On a green willow tree.

8. For the leaves, they will wither,
   And the roots, they will die,
   And your true love will leave you,
   And you'll never know why.

Over the River and Through the Woods

Traditional

First note

Brightly

1. O - ver the riv - er and thro' the woods, to
2. O - ver the riv - er and thro' the woods, to
3. O - ver the riv - er and thro' the woods, and

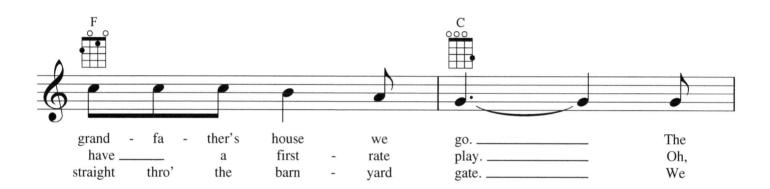

grand - fa - ther's house we go. _____ The
have _____ a first - rate play. _____ Oh,
straight thro' the barn - yard gate. _____ We

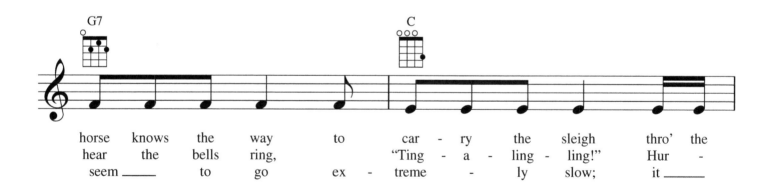

horse knows the way to car - ry the sleigh thro' the
hear the bells ring, "Ting - a - ling - ling!" Hur -
seem _____ to go ex - treme - ly slow; it _____

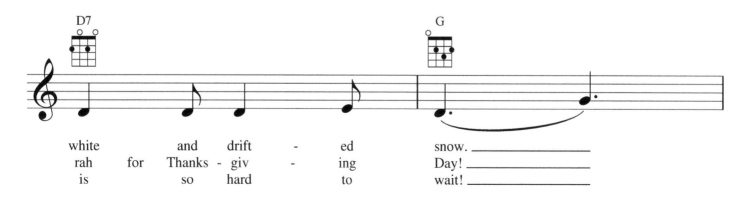

white and drift - ed snow. _____
rah for Thanks - giv - ing Day! _____
is so hard to wait! _____

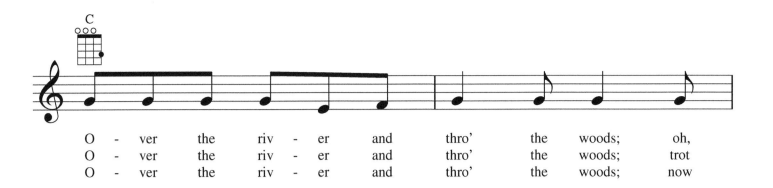

O	-	ver	the	riv	-	er	and	thro'	the	woods;	oh,
O	-	ver	the	riv	-	er	and	thro'	the	woods;	trot
O	-	ver	the	riv	-	er	and	thro'	the	woods;	now

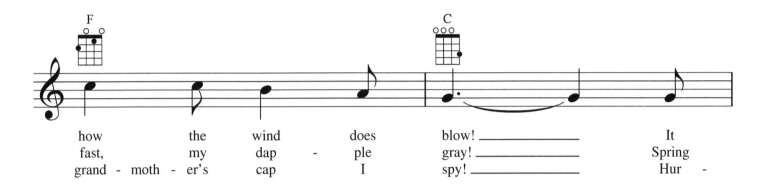

how	the	wind	does	blow! _____	It
fast,	my	dap	-	ple	gray! _____	Spring
grand	- moth	- er's	cap	I	spy! _____	Hur	-

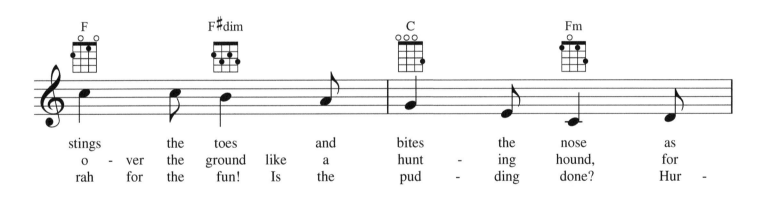

stings	the	toes	and	bites	the	nose	as
o	- ver	the	ground	like	a	hunt	- ing	hound,	as	for
rah	for	the	fun!	Is	the	pud	- ding	done?	Hur	-

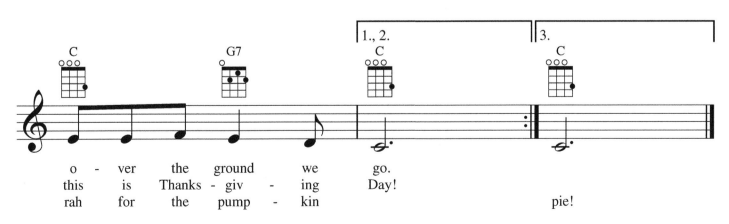

o	- ver	the	ground	we	go.
this	is	Thanks	- giv	- ing	Day!
rah	for	the	pump	- kin	pie!

Peanut Sat on a Railroad Track

Traditional

The Red River Valley

Traditional American Cowboy Song

First note

Slowly

1. Come and sit by my side if you love me.
2. Won't you think of this val - ley you're leav - ing,
3. From this val - ley they say you are go - ing.
4. I have prom - ised you, dar - ling, that nev - er

Do not has - ten to bid me a -
oh, how lone - ly, how sad it will
When you go, may your dar - ling go,
will a word from my lips cause you

dieu.
be.
too?
pain.
But re - mem - ber the
Oh, think of the
Would you leave her be -
And my life, it will

Red Riv - er Val - ley, and the
fond heart you're break - ing, and the
hind un - pro - tect - ed when she
be yours for - ev - er, if you

cow - boy that loves you so true.
grief you are caus - ing me.
loves no oth - er but you?
on - ly will love me a - gain.

Rock Island Line

Railroad Song

First note

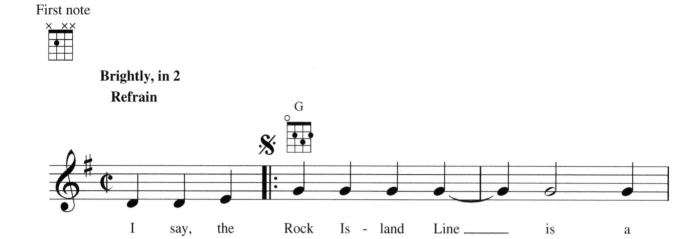

Brightly, in 2
Refrain

I say, the Rock Is - land Line _____ is a

might - y good road. _____ I say, the Rock Is - land Line _

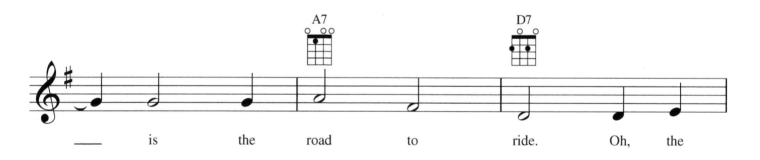

_ is the road to ride. Oh, the

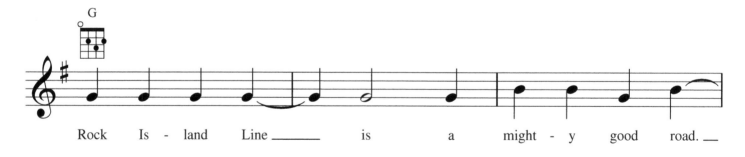

Rock Is - land Line _____ is a might - y good road. _

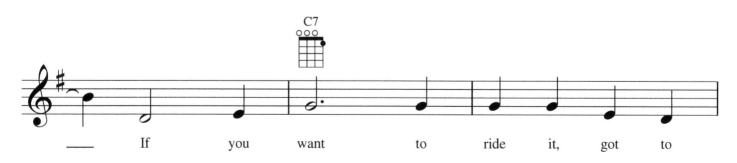

_ If you want to ride it, got to

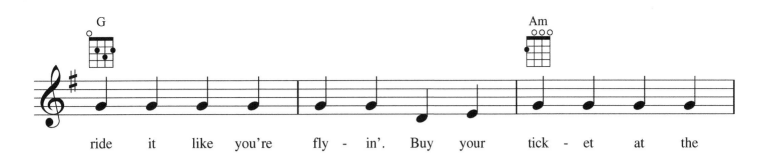

ride it like you're fly - in'. Buy your tick - et at the

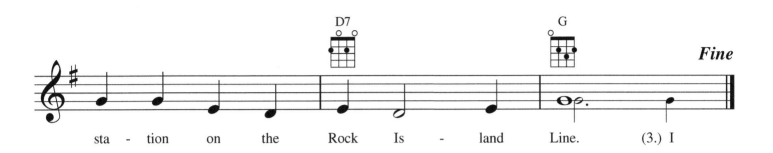

Fine

sta - tion on the Rock Is - land Line.   (3.) I

Verse

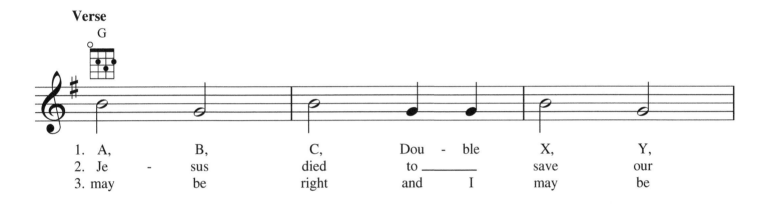

1. A,   B,   C,   Dou - ble   X,   Y,
2. Je - sus   died   to ____   save   our
3. may   be   right   and   I   may   be

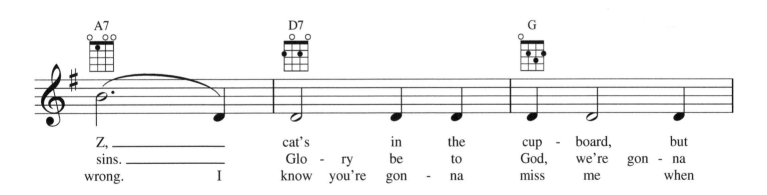

Z, _____   cat's   in   the   cup - board,   but
sins. _____   Glo - ry   be   to   God,   we're gon - na
wrong.   I   know   you're gon - na   miss   me   when

| 1., 2. | 3. |

D.S. al Fine

he can't see me. ____   I say, the
see Him a - gain. ____   I say, the
I ____ have gone. __   ____ I say, the

Rock-A-My Soul

African-American Spiritual

First note

Brightly
Refrain

Oh, rock - a - my soul __ in the bos - om of A - bra - ham,

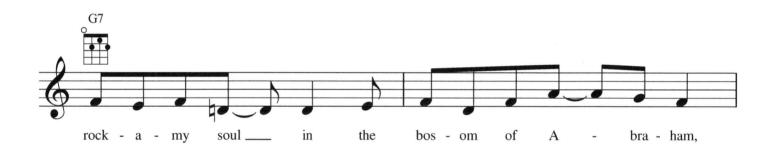

rock - a - my soul __ in the bos - om of A - bra - ham,

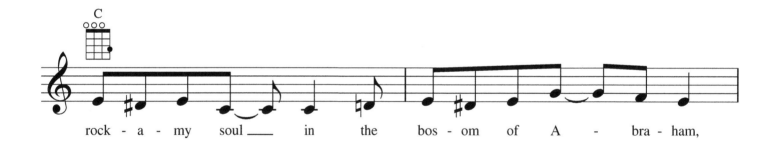

rock - a - my soul __ in the bos - om of A - bra - ham,

oh, rock - a - my soul.

1. When
2. When
3. I
4. The

Verse

I went down to the val - ley to pray,
I came home from the val - ley at night,
felt so sad on the morn - ing be - fore,
sun shines bright on the cloud - i - est day,

oh, rock - a - my soul. My
oh, rock - a - my soul. I
oh, rock - a - my soul. I
oh, rock - a - my soul. A

soul got hap - py and I stayed all day,
knew that ev - 'ry - thing would be al - right,
found the peace that I was look - ing for,
prayer is all you need to light your way,

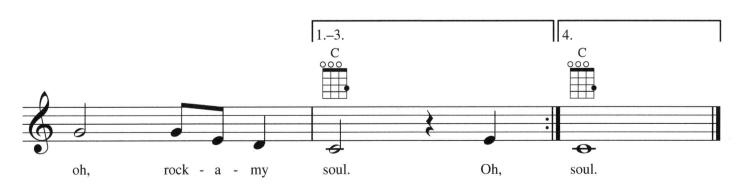

oh, rock - a - my soul. Oh, soul.

Row, Row, Row Your Boat

Traditional

First note

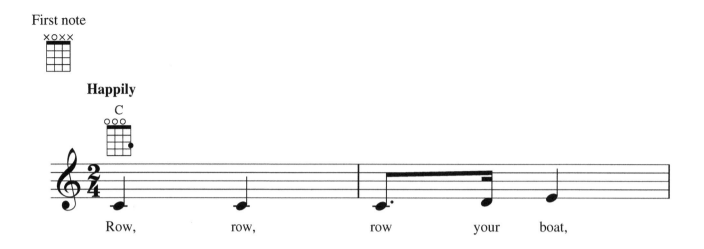

Happily

Row,   row,   row   your   boat,

gen - tly   down   the   stream.

Mer - ri - ly,   mer - ri - ly,   mer - ri - ly,   mer - ri - ly,

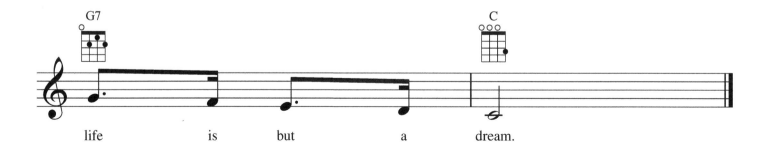

life   is   but   a   dream.

She'll Be Comin' 'Round the Mountain

Traditional

Scarborough Fair

Traditional English

First note

Moderately and freely

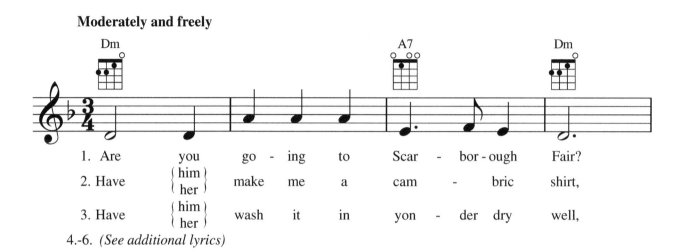

1. Are you go - ing to Scar - bor - ough Fair?
2. Have { him her } make me a cam - bric shirt,
3. Have { him her } wash it in yon - der dry well,

4.-6. *(See additional lyrics)*

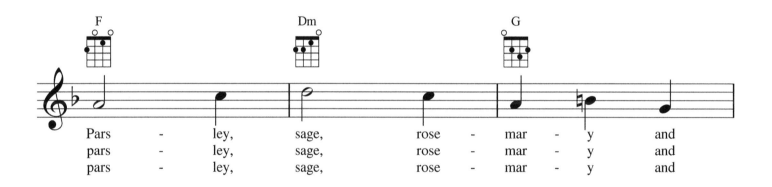

Pars - ley, sage, rose - mar - y and
pars - ley, sage, rose - mar - y and
pars - ley, sage, rose - mar - y and

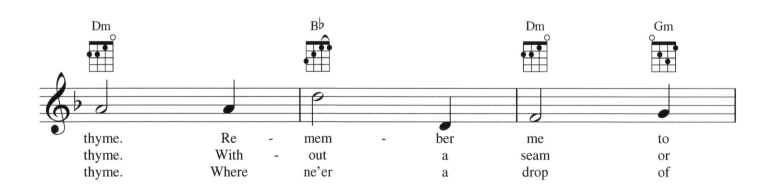

thyme. Re - mem - ber me to
thyme. With - out a seam or
thyme. Where ne'er a drop of

one	who	lives	there,	_____	for	once	{ he } { she }
fine	nee	- dle	- work,	_____	and	then	{ he'll } { she'll }
wa	- ter	e'er	fell,	_____	and	then	{ he'll } { she'll }

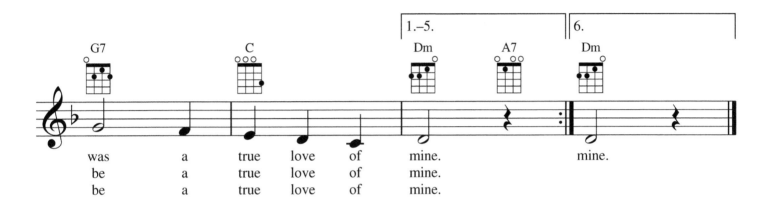

was	a	true	love	of	mine.		mine.
be	a	true	love	of	mine.		
be	a	true	love	of	mine.		

Additional Lyrics

4. Have him (her) find me an acre of land,
   Parsley, sage, rosemary and thyme.
   Between the sea and over the sand,
   And then he'll (she'll) be a true love of mine.

5. Plow the land with the horn of a lamb,
   Parsley, sage, rosemary and thyme.
   Then sow some seeds from north of the dam,
   And then he'll (she'll) be a true love of mine.

6. If he (she) tells me he (she) can't, I'll reply:
   Parsley, sage, rosemary and thyme.
   Let me know that at least he (she) will try,
   And then he'll (she'll) be a true love of mine.

School Days
(When We Were a Couple of Kids)

Words by Will D. Cobb
Music by Gus Edwards

First note

Waltz tempo

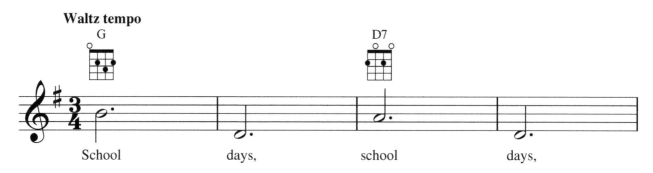

School   days,   school   days,

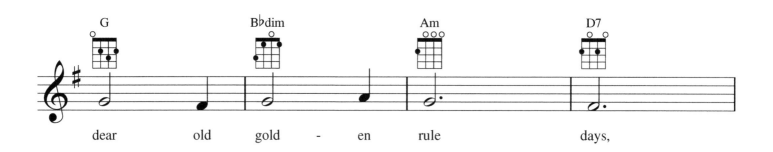

dear   old   gold - en   rule   days,

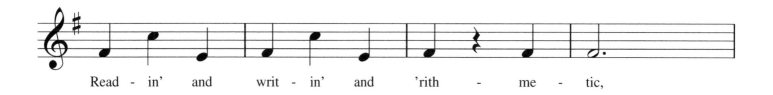

Read - in'   and   writ - in'   and   'rith - me - tic,

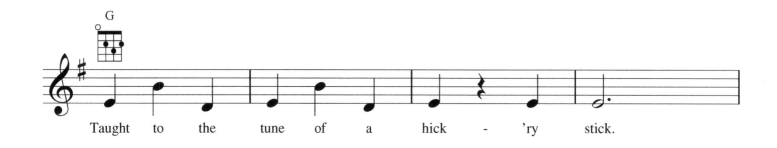

Taught   to   the   tune   of   a   hick - 'ry   stick.

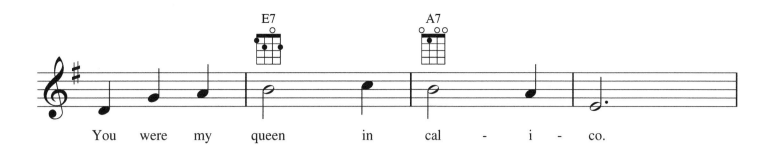

You were my queen in cal - i - co.

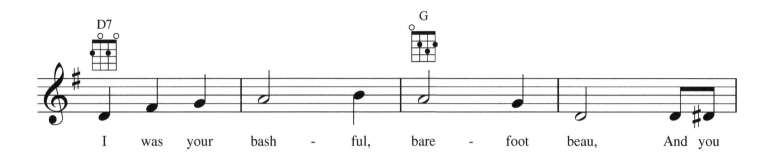

I was your bash - ful, bare - foot beau, And you

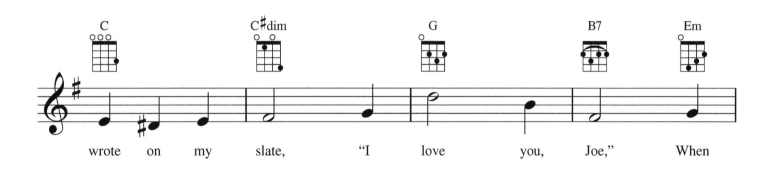

wrote on my slate, "I love you, Joe," When

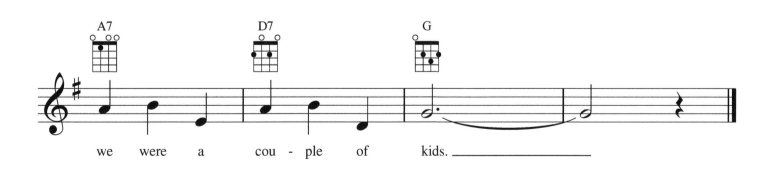

we were a cou - ple of kids. _____

She Wore a Yellow Ribbon

Words and Music by George A. Norton

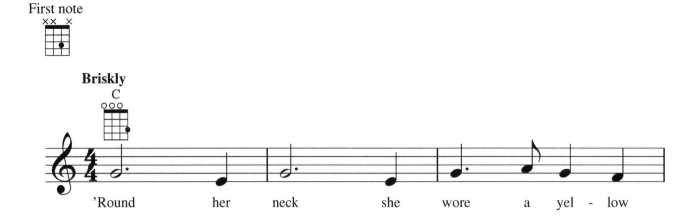

'Round her neck she wore a yel - low

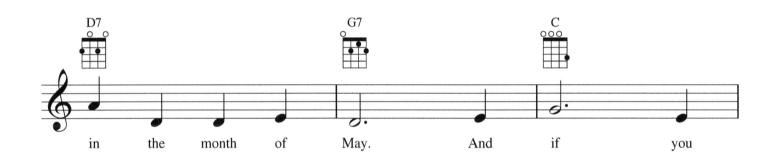

rib - bon; she wore it in the spring - time and

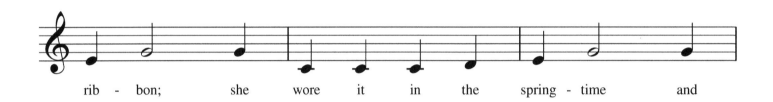

in the month of May. And if you

asked her why the heck she wore it, she

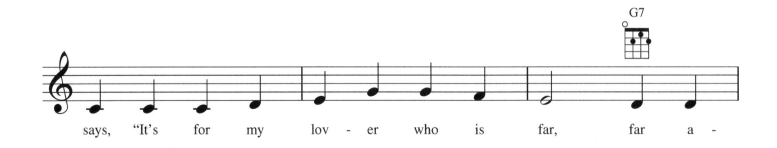

says, "It's for my lov - er who is far, far a -

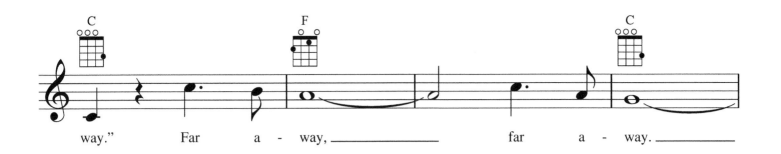

way." Far a - way, _____ far a - way. _____

_____ She wore it for her lov - er far a -

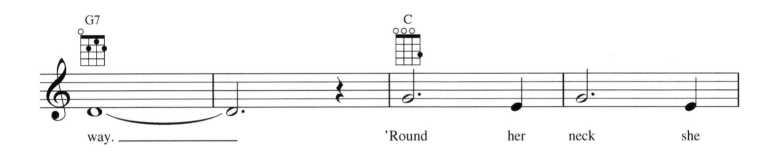

way. _____ 'Round her neck she

wore a yel - low rib - bon; she wore it for her

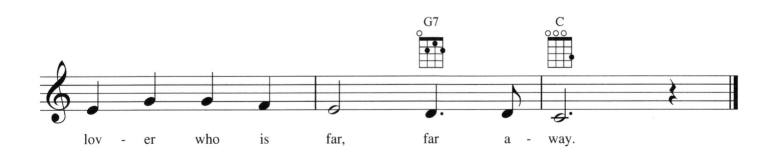

lov - er who is far, far a - way.

Shenandoah

American Folksong

First note

Gently

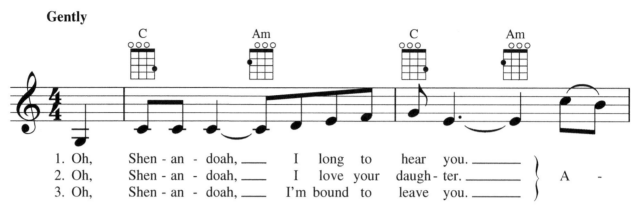

1. Oh, Shen - an - doah, _____ I long to hear you. _____
2. Oh, Shen - an - doah, _____ I love your daugh - ter. _____
3. Oh, Shen - an - doah, _____ I'm bound to leave you. _____

A -

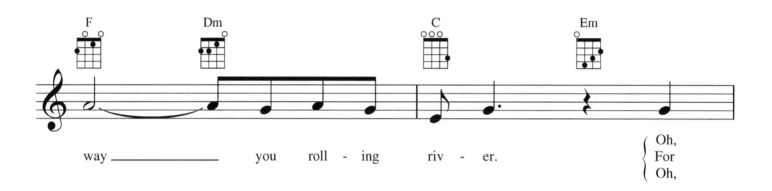

way _____ you roll - ing riv - er.

{ Oh,
{ For
{ Oh,

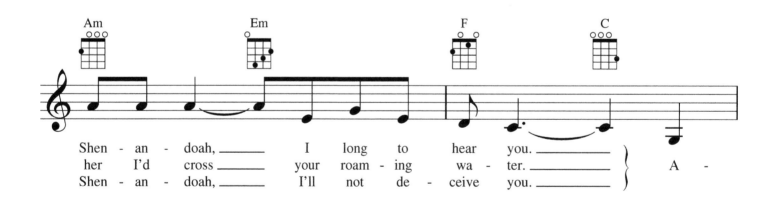

Shen - an - doah, _____ I long to hear you. _____
her I'd cross _____ your roam - ing wa - ter. _____
Shen - an - doah, _____ I'll not de - ceive you. _____

A -

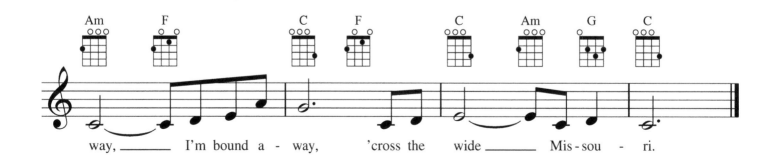

way, _____ I'm bound a - way, 'cross the wide _____ Mis - sou - ri.

Sometimes I Feel Like a Motherless Child

African-American Spiritual

First note

Slowly

1. Some-times I feel like a moth-er-less child. ____
2. Some-times I feel like I'm al - most gone. ____

Some - times I feel like a moth-er-less child. ____
Some - times I feel like I'm al - most gone. ____

Some - times I feel like a moth-er-less child, ____
Some - times I feel like I'm al - most gone, ____ a

long way ____ from home, _____ a

long way ____ from home. ____

Swing Low, Sweet Chariot

Traditional Spiritual

First note

Moderately slow, in 2
Refrain

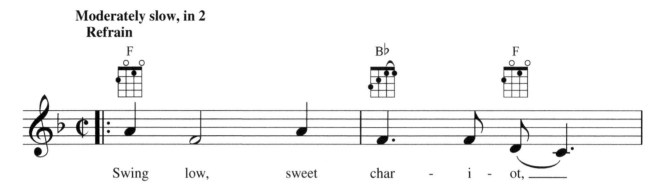

Swing   low,   sweet   char - i - ot, _____

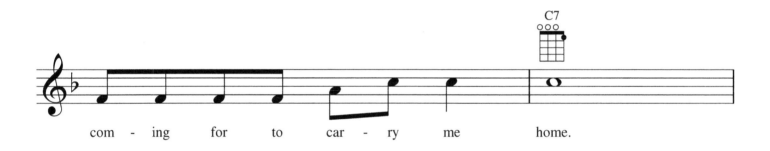

com - ing   for   to   car - ry   me   home.

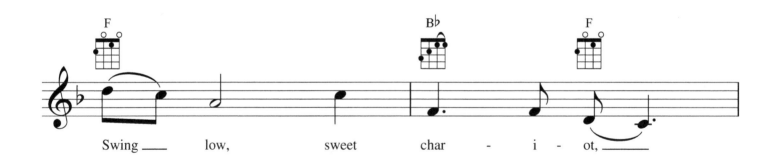

Swing ____ low,   sweet   char - i - ot, _____

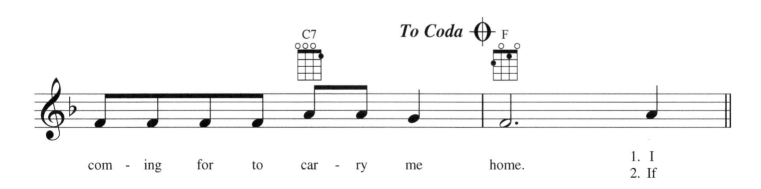

com - ing   for   to   car - ry   me   home.

1. I
2. If

Verse

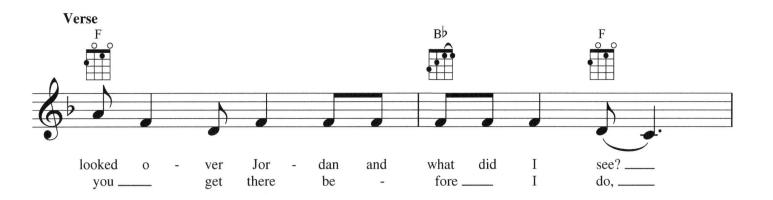

looked o - ver Jor - dan and what did I see? ____
you ____ get there be - fore ____ I do, ____

com - ing for to car - ry me home, a
com - ing for to car - ry me home, tell

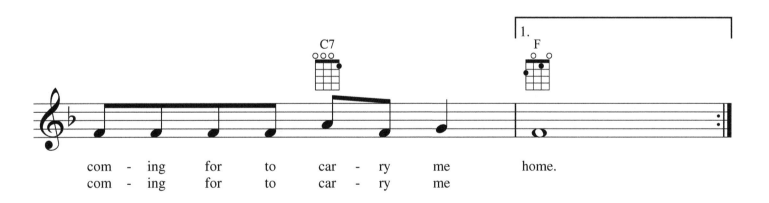

band ____ of an - gels com - ing af - ter me, ____
all ____ my friends I'm com - ing, ____ too, ____

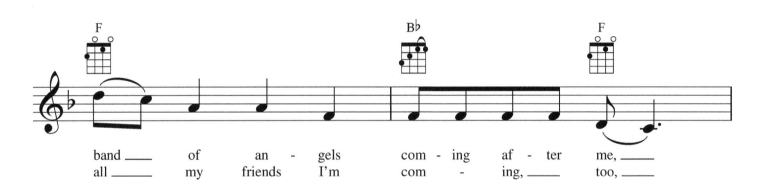

1.

com - ing for to car - ry me home.
com - ing for to car - ry me

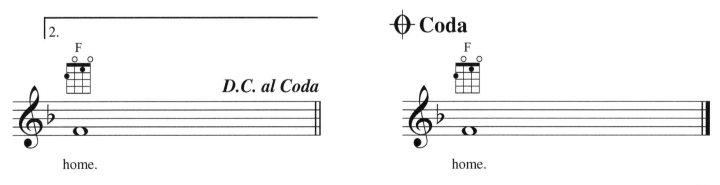

2.

D.C. al Coda

home.

$\oplus$ **Coda**

home.

83

Take Me Out to the Ball Game

Words by Jack Norworth
Music by Albert von Tilzer

First note

Brightly

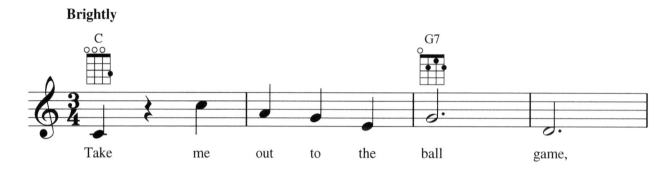

Take me out to the ball game,

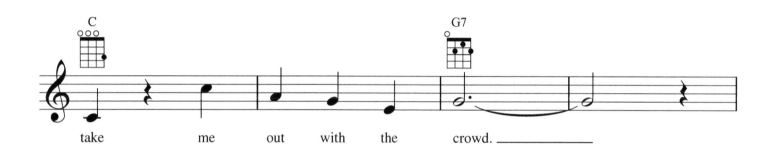

take me out with the crowd. _____

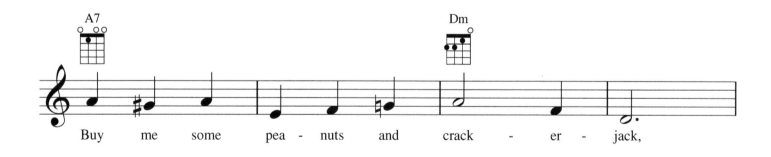

Buy me some pea - nuts and crack - er - jack,

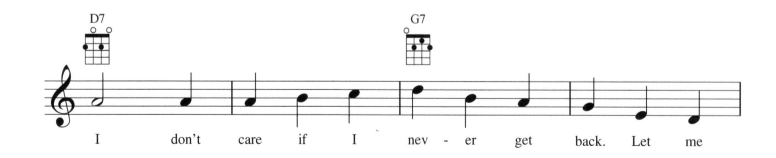

I don't care if I nev - er get back. Let me

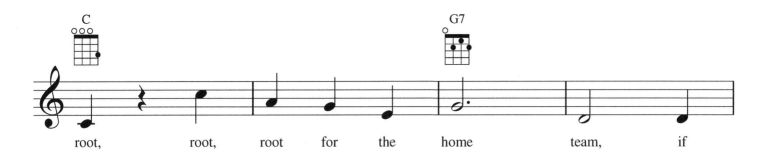

root,   root,   root   for   the   home   team,   if

they   don't   win   it's   a   shame. _____   For   it's

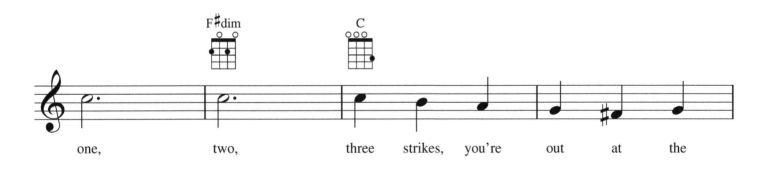

one,   two,   three   strikes,   you're   out   at   the

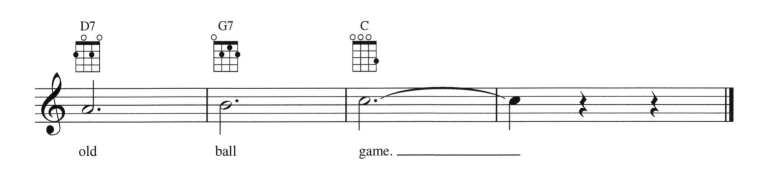

old   ball   game. _____

There Is a Tavern in the Town

Traditional Drinking Song

Refrain

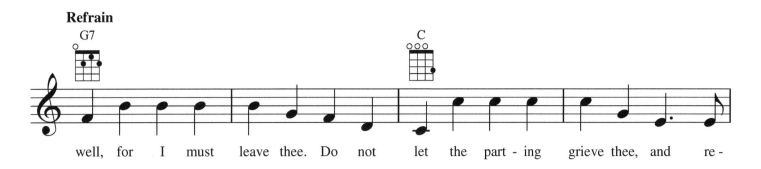

well, for I must leave thee. Do not let the part - ing grieve thee, and re -

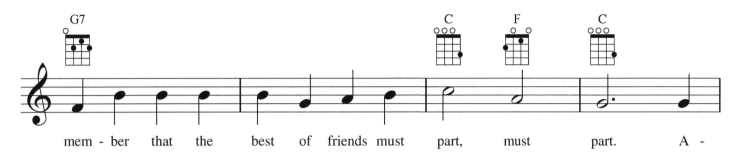

mem - ber that the best of friends must part, must part. A -

dieu, a - dieu, kind friends, a - dieu, a - dieu, a - dieu. I

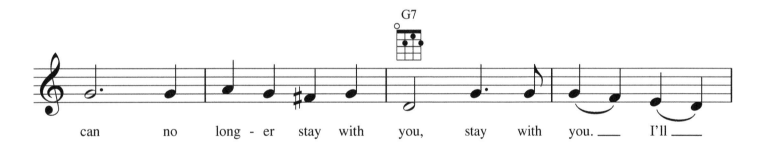

can no long - er stay with you, stay with you. ___ I'll ___

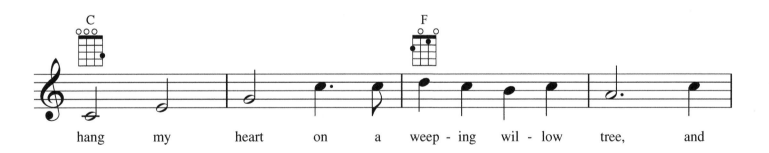

hang my heart on a weep - ing wil - low tree, and

may the world go well with thee. _____

This Old Man

Traditional

First note

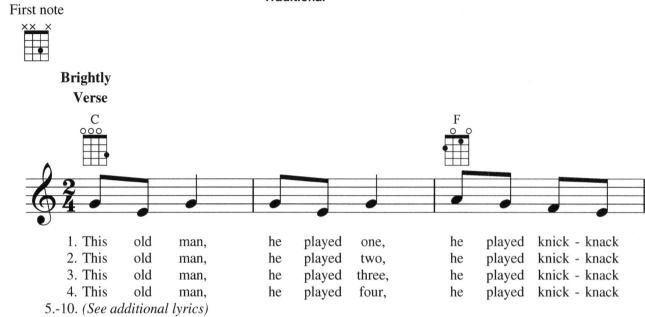

Brightly

Verse

1. This old man, he played one, he played knick - knack
2. This old man, he played two, he played knick - knack
3. This old man, he played three, he played knick - knack
4. This old man, he played four, he played knick - knack

5.-10. *(See additional lyrics)*

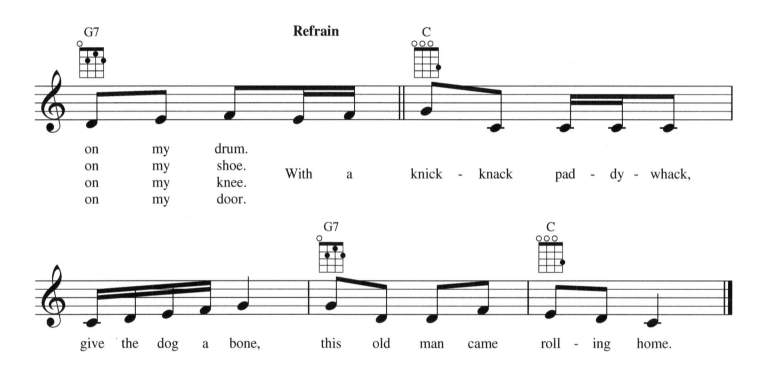

on my drum.
on my shoe.
on my knee.
on my door.

Refrain With a knick - knack pad - dy - whack,

give the dog a bone, this old man came roll - ing home.

Additional Lyrics

5. This old man, he played five,
   He played knick-knack on my hive.
   Refrain

6. This old man, he played six,
   He played knick-knack on my sticks.
   Refrain

7. This old man, he played seven,
   He played knick-knack up to heaven.
   Refrain

8. This old man, he played eight,
   He played knick-knack at the gate.
   Refrain

9. This old man, he played nine,
   He played knick-knack on my line.
   Refrain

10. This old man, he played ten,
    He played knick-knack over again.
    Refrain

We Gather Together

Words from *Nederlandtsch Gedenckclanck*
Translated by Theodore Baker
Netherlands Folk Melody
Arranged by Edward Kremser

First note

Flowing

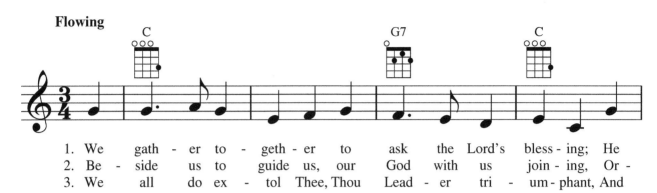

1. We gath - er to - geth - er to ask the Lord's bless - ing; He
2. Be - side us to guide us, our God with us join - ing, Or -
3. We all do ex - tol Thee, Thou Lead - er tri - um - phant, And

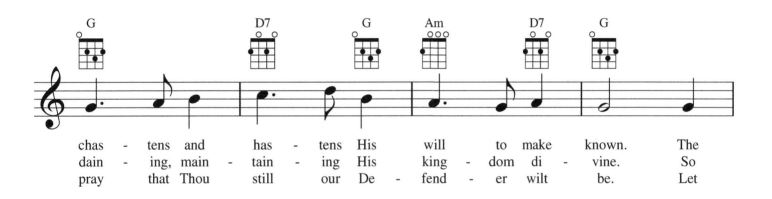

chas - tens and has - tens His will to make known. The
dain - ing, main - tain - ing His king - dom di - vine. So
pray that Thou still our De - fend - er wilt be. Let

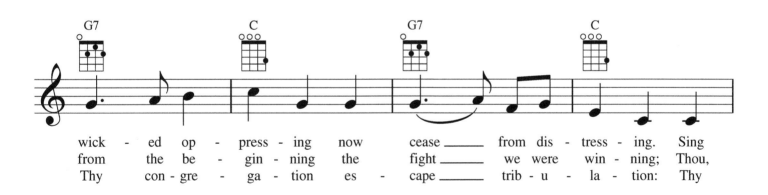

wick - ed op - press - ing now cease _____ from dis - tress - ing. Sing
from the be - gin - ning the fight _____ we were win - ning; Thou,
Thy con - gre - ga - tion es - cape _____ trib - u - la - tion: Thy

prais - es to His name _____ He for - gets not His own.
Lord, wast at our side, _____ all _____ glo - ry be Thine!
name be ev - er praised! _____ O _____ Lord, make us free!

When the Saints Go Marching In

Words by Katherine E. Purvis
Music by James M. Black

Yankee Doodle

Traditional

Additional Lyrics

4. And then the feathers on his hat,
They looked so 'tarnel fine, ah!
I wanted peskily to get
To give to me Jemima.
Chorus

5. We saw a little barrel, too,
The heads were made of leather.
They knocked on it with little clubs
And called the folks together.
Chorus

6. And there they'd fife away like fun,
And play on cornstalk fiddles.
And some had ribbons red as blood
All bound around their middles.
Chorus

The Yellow Rose of Texas

Words and Music by J.K., 1858

Chorus

nev - er - more will part. ⎫
not to leave her so. ⎬ She's the sweet-est rose of
mine for - ev - er - more. ⎭

col - or this fel - low ev - er knew. Her

eyes are bright as dia - monds, they spar - kle like the

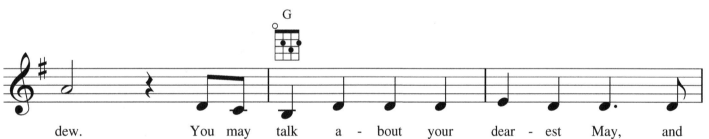

dew. You may talk a - bout your dear - est May, and

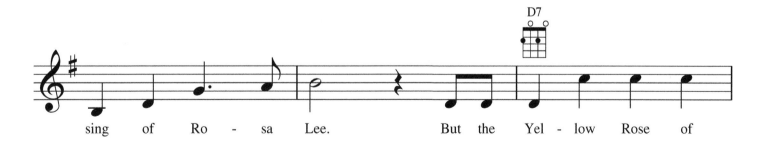

sing of Ro - sa Lee. But the Yel - low Rose of

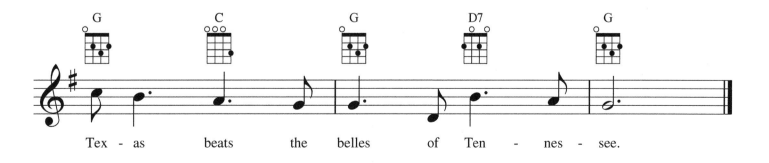

Tex - as beats the belles of Ten - nes - see.

93

The Best Collections for Ukulele

The Best Songs Ever

70 songs have now been arranged for ukulele. Includes: Always • Bohemian Rhapsody • Memory • My Favorite Things • Over the Rainbow • Piano Man • What a Wonderful World • Yesterday • You Raise Me Up • and more.

00282413........$17.99

Campfire Songs for Ukulele

30 favorites to sing as you roast marshmallows and strum your uke around the campfire. Includes: God Bless the U.S.A. • Hallelujah • The House of the Rising Sun • I Walk the Line • Puff the Magic Dragon • Wagon Wheel • You Are My Sunshine • and more.

00129170 ....$14.99

The Daily Ukulele

arr. Liz and Jim Beloff
Strum a different song everyday with easy arrangements of 365 of your favorite songs in one big songbook! Includes favorites by the Beatles, Beach Boys, and Bob Dylan, folk songs, pop songs, kids' songs, Christmas carols, and Broadway and Hollywood tunes, all with a spiral binding for ease of use.

00240356 Original Edition.........$39.99
00240681 Leap Year Edition $39.99
00119270 Portable Edition $37.50

Disney Hits for Ukulele

Play 23 of your favorite Disney songs on your ukulele. Includes: The Bare Necessities • Cruella De Vil • Do You Want to Build a Snowman? • Kiss the Girl • Lava • Let It Go • Once upon a Dream • A Whole New World • and more.

00151250 ....$16.99

Also available:

00291547 **Disney Fun Songs for Ukulele** ...$16.99
00701708 **Disney Songs for Ukulele**.......$14.99
00334696 **First 50 Disney Songs on Ukulele** .$16.99

First 50 Songs You Should Play on Ukulele

An amazing collec-tion of 50 accessible, must-know favorites: Edelweiss • Hey, Soul Sister • I Walk the Line • I'm Yours • Imagine • Over the Rainbow • Peaceful Easy Feeling • The Rainbow Connection • Riptide • more.

00149250 ....$16.99

Also available:

00292082 **First 50 Melodies on Ukulele** ...$15.99
00289029 **First 50 Songs on Solo Ukulele**..$15.99
00347437 **First 50 Songs to Strum on Uke** .$16.99

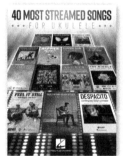

40 Most Streamed Songs for Ukulele

40 top hits that sound great on uke! Includes: Despacito • Feel It Still • Girls like You • Happier • Havana • High Hopes • The Middle • Perfect • 7 Rings • Shallow • Shape of You • Something Just like This • Stay • Sucker • Sunflower • Sweet but Psycho • Thank U, Next • There's Nothing Holdin' Me Back • Without Me • and more!

00298113 ....$17.99

The 4 Chord Songbook

With just 4 chords, you can play 50 hot songs on your ukulele! Songs include: Brown Eyed Girl • Do Wah Diddy Diddy • Hey Ya! • Ho Hey • Jessie's Girl • Let It Be • One Love • Stand by Me • Toes • With or Without You • and many more.

00142050........$16.99

Also available:

00141143 **The 3-Chord Songbook**........$16.99

Pop Songs for Kids

30 easy pop favorites for kids to play on uke, including: Brave • Can't Stop the Feeling! • Feel It Still • Fight Song • Happy • Havana • House of Gold • How Far I'll Go • Let It Go • Remember Me (Ernesto de la Cruz) • Rewrite the Stars • Roar • Shake It Off • Story of My Life • What Makes You Beautiful • and more.

00284415 ....$16.99

Simple Songs for Ukulele

50 favorites for standard G-C-E-A ukulele tuning, including: All Along the Watchtower • Can't Help Falling in Love • Don't Worry, Be Happy • Ho Hey • I'm Yours • King of the Road • Sweet Home Alabama • You Are My Sunshine • and more.

00156815.......$14.99

Also available:

00276644 **More Simple Songs for Ukulele** .$14.99

Top Hits of 2020

18 uke-friendly tunes of 2020 are featured in this collection of melody, lyric and chord arrangements in standard G-C-E-A tuning. Includes: Adore You (Harry Styles) • Before You Go (Lewis Capaldi) • Cardigan (Taylor Swift) • Daisies (Katy Perry) • I Dare You (Kelly Clarkson) • Level of Concern (twenty one pilots) • No Time to Die (Billie Eilish) • Rain on Me (Lady Gaga feat. Ariana Grande) • Say So (Doja Cat) • and more.

00355553 ....$14.99

Also available:

00302274 **Top Hits of 2019** $14.99

Ukulele: The Most Requested Songs

Strum & Sing Series
Cherry Lane Music
Nearly 50 favorites all expertly arranged for ukulele! Includes: Bubbly • Build Me Up, Buttercup • Cecilia • Georgia on My Mind • Kokomo • L-O-V-E • Your Body Is a Wonderland • and more.

02501453 ....$14.99

The Ultimate Ukulele Fake Book

Uke enthusiasts will love this giant, spiral-bound collection of over 400 songs for uke! Includes: Crazy • Dancing Queen • Downtown • Fields of Gold • Happy • Hey Jude • 7 Years • Summertime • Thinking Out Loud • Thriller • Wagon Wheel • and more.

00175500 9" x 12" Edition $45.00
00319997 5.5" x 8.5" Edition $39.99

HAL•LEONARD® UKULELE PLAY-ALONG

AUDIO ACCESS INCLUDED

Now you can play your favorite songs on your uke with great-sounding backing tracks to help you sound like a bona fide pro! The audio also features playback tools so you can adjust the tempo without changing the pitch and loop challenging parts.

1. POP HITS
00701451 Book/CD Pack..............$15.99

2. UKE CLASSICS
00701452 Book/CD Pack..............$15.99

3. HAWAIIAN FAVORITES
00701453 Book/Online Audio..........$14.99

4. CHILDREN'S SONGS
00701454 Book/Online Audio..........$14.99

5. CHRISTMAS SONGS
00701696 Book/CD Pack..............$12.99

6. LENNON & MCCARTNEY
00701723 Book/Online Audio..........$12.99

7. DISNEY FAVORITES
00701724 Book/Online Audio..........$12.99

8. CHART HITS
00701745 Book/CD Pack..............$15.99

9. THE SOUND OF MUSIC
00701784 Book/CD Pack..............$14.99

10. MOTOWN
00701964 Book/CD Pack..............$12.99

11. CHRISTMAS STRUMMING
00702458 Book/Online Audio..........$12.99

12. BLUEGRASS FAVORITES
00702584 Book/CD Pack..............$12.99

13. UKULELE SONGS
00702599 Book/CD Pack..............$12.99

14. JOHNNY CASH
00702615 Book/CD Pack..............$15.99

15. COUNTRY CLASSICS
00702834 Book/CD Pack..............$12.99

16. STANDARDS
00702835 Book/CD Pack..............$12.99

17. POP STANDARDS
00702836 Book/CD Pack..............$12.99

18. IRISH SONGS
00703086 Book/Online Audio..........$12.99

19. BLUES STANDARDS
00703087 Book/CD Pack..............$12.99

20. FOLK POP ROCK
00703088 Book/CD Pack..............$12.99

21. HAWAIIAN CLASSICS
00703097 Book/CD Pack..............$12.99

22. ISLAND SONGS
00703098 Book/CD Pack..............$12.99

23. TAYLOR SWIFT – 2ND EDITION
00221966 Book/Online Audio..........$16.99

24. WINTER WONDERLAND
00101871 Book/CD Pack..............$12.99

25. GREEN DAY
00110398 Book/CD Pack..............$14.99

26. BOB MARLEY
00110399 Book/Online Audio..........$14.99

27. TIN PAN ALLEY
00116358 Book/CD Pack..............$12.99

28. STEVIE WONDER
00116736 Book/CD Pack..............$14.99

29. OVER THE RAINBOW & OTHER FAVORITES
00117076 Book/Online Audio..........$14.99

30. ACOUSTIC SONGS
00122336 Book/CD Pack..............$14.99

31. JASON MRAZ
00124166 Book/CD Pack..............$14.99

32. TOP DOWNLOADS
00127507 Book/CD Pack..............$14.99

33. CLASSICAL THEMES
00127892 Book/Online Audio..........$14.99

34. CHRISTMAS HITS
00128602 Book/CD Pack..............$14.99

35. SONGS FOR BEGINNERS
00129009 Book/Online Audio..........$14.99

36. ELVIS PRESLEY HAWAII
00138199 Book/Online Audio..........$14.99

37. LATIN
00141191 Book/Online Audio..........$14.99

38. JAZZ
00141192 Book/Online Audio..........$14.99

39. GYPSY JAZZ
00146559 Book/Online Audio..........$14.99

40. TODAY'S HITS
00160845 Book/Online Audio..........$14.99

Prices, contents, and availability subject to change without notice.

HAL•LEONARD®
www.halleonard.com

0719
483